THE UNIVERSITY
of EDINBURGH

from Arthur's Seat

creative writing from the University of Edinburgh

2016

from Arthur's Seat

First published by Egg Box Publishing 2016
in partnership with the University of Edinburgh

A CIP record for this book is available from the British Library

Design by Ignacio B. Peña

Typeset in Charter, 10 pt

Printed and bound in the UK by Imprint Digital

Distributed by Central Books

ISBN: 978-1-911343-10-3

from Arthur's Seat

editorial team

Alyson Kissner
Amani Al-Remal
Angela L. Hicks
Ignacio B. Peña
Kelly Pierce
Lori Sheirich

readers

C.M.A. Hudson   Krystal Foster   Mark Wightman

cover artwork

Alice Gray

section artwork

Heledd Owen

writer-in-residence

Sam Riviere

special thanks

Alan Gillis   Allyson Stack   Beth Cochrane
Danny Leyland   Jane McKie   Ricky Brown
Robert Alan Jamieson   Tracey Emerson

table of contents

poetry

competition winners

foreword

'From Arthur's Seat' – to those unfamiliar with the city of Edinburgh, the phrase may conjure the indistinct image of an ancient fabled king, a legendary presence sat upon a throne issuing edicts to those who make up his court. To those who know the city, the image is immediately clear. It is the wild that lies in the heart of the Scottish capital, the volcanic hill visible to citizens through the seasons, its colours changing, yet a familiar constant. And if recorded human history on its slopes dates as far back as the epic Brythonic poem, 'The Goddodin', in which the great King Arthur is indeed mentioned, the mount itself is older by far and has silently witnessed ages far older than legend. The wanderer, passing over its slopes, cannot help but be affected by a sense of this long history, this constancy in the middle of human endeavour; the writer even more so.

From the old university buildings in the heart of the city's Southside, Arthur's Seat appears as the lion *couchant*; from Arthur's Seat, the city stretches out on all sides, from the Pentland Hills to the south, to the Firth of Forth to the north. Traffic buzzes around its base, but the lion is unmoved: only the slightest incursions into its sanctuary have been made, and those who live in its shadows are grateful for that, for the island of wilderness it provides, and the vision afforded by climbing to its heights. It is a place to inspire.

The city has long been a place of learning, of thought, of literature, and of publishing. Through its streets, over many centuries, philosophers and poets, novelists, dramatists and journalists, have walked in the domain of this lion *couchant*, engaged in the art of composition, aware of the tradition they themselves help to extend. Edinburgh was the first UNESCO World City of Literature and has been home to some of the world's most notable and successful authors over the long years of its existence. The university's list of literary alumni, too, is a proud one. Even before the emergence of 'Creative Writing' as an academic subject, writers congregated here, shared work-in-progress, published magazines and anthologies, reviewed books and so on. And now, each year, from the far reaches of the world, those who would be writers come to spend time focusing on their chosen art, to develop their skills in this inspiring, supportive atmosphere – to pass through what someone once called the tempering forge of workshop.

In the volume before you now, you will find some of the many and varied vistas which writers at the University of Edinburgh have sighted from this vantage point during the year 2015-16. These glimpses of elsewhere create a sampler full of treasures and delights to be savoured at leisure. The range of voice and tone, of form and content, makes for kaleidoscopic entertainment. Blessed with the gift of imagination, their views have stretched far beyond the city itself, across land and sea and time to reach distant settings in the USA, to fictional places of great invention such as Yiddishland or a second Earth – and even, Edinburghers might say with a wink, to Glasgow. 'From Arthur's Seat', the world is visible, and other worlds beyond it.

Robert Alan Jamieson
Senior Lecturer
The University of Edinburgh

fiction

Amani Al-Remal

Give Me Your Everything

Of all things, the true things to know about me—to fix in your head about me as this goes on—are that I was twenty-four years old, this was my first relationship and they were a Blurb-Beauty who wasn't fully sharp to that fact. I was out-of-my-wits, out-of-my-soul lucky to have met them, to have the chance to have them.

With this in mind, I felt I should give this the best of what I had. And my best, so you know, is my words.

So, feeling this, the Blurb-Beauty—from now on, I'll call them Seren—and I decided to do that, just that.

What I liked about Seren was that they were precisely-spoken. When I suggested scripting our interactions and sending them to each other to read and approve in advance, they nodded and said that 'would be all we needed to do'.

I mailed them the first script three days after that. What follows is an excerpt:

[The scene is your current partner's apartment. He has cooked mushroom ravioli/spinach and feta pizza because he is—supportively—aware of your vegetarianism. Today is the day of your fifth date, and seventh encounter non-romantically. You are both dressed in accordance with this.]

Me: Well, hello again, Seren. It's nice to see you again.
Seren: Hi. Nice to be here.
Me: Well, well, come in, then! Please don't loiter out there. It's bitterly cold.
Seren: Thank you for that. I was beginning to feel a bit chilly, in truth.
Me: Come in, come in now.
Seren: My, *[in a way that indicates they are not in tacit compliance with traditional gender roles]* what you've cooked smells quite delicious and I'm glad of that.
Me: *[appreciating that they have shown an awareness of and an aversion to imbibed sexism]* Thank you, that's truly sweet of you to say.

[They move into the living room]

Seren: *[noting the simple yet tasteful furnishings]* This is a lovely room. So effectively furnished.

Me: *[blushing lightly, appropriately]* Thanks, Seren. Shall we have dinner now?

Seren: That would be perfect.

In the scripting was our rhythm.

Seren's drafts confounded me: slappingly direct but with a something too-real, too-near that seemed to plump the paper. Here, for example, is an excerpt from the third one they wrote:

You: *[you'll look incredible]* Hi, Seren.

Me: Hi.

You: So, what's the plan for tonight?

Me: We eat dinner, watch a film, take a stroll, then go back to my place.

You: Right and yes. OK.

I didn't hear from Seren after that for two weeks. I sent them five scripts, with the date, time and place written on the last page, as emboldened and underlined as always.

They came to the fifth one holding a bouquet of lilies. I was supposed to have brought a bouquet of red roses to the fourth one. They ran parallel with their nose, the cleft—somehow surrendering, graceless—in their chin. Their face seemed to grow out of the shrill whiteness.

And then it was growing, and growing more still. All of them sprung and stretched and they were now about ten feet high.

They were a Full Beauty now and oh the wonder of them. The bouquet of lilies flaked out of their hands onto my eyelashes, my shoulders, my hands. They looked down at me.

'How long have you known?'

'That - that you were - '

'A Blurb-Beauty. Yes.'

'From the start.'

'And you didn't think to tell me?'

'I didn't want to.'

They hunched their shoulders slightly and folded their arms—their immense, immense arms—across their chest.

'You did all this. With your scripts and your planning. You—you took me from myself.'

'Maybe.'

‘I can’t begin anything with anyone, ever again, now. You know that?’

‘I know. I’m sorry.’

‘No. You’re not.’

We were silent for some minutes. Then their clothes began to change: the bottoms lengthened and widened, their t-shirt became its full-sleeved counterpart. Both were dove white. A small-brimmed hat appeared on their head, and their right hand gripped around a lace umbrella.

Its spokes burned blue, then red. Their finger lightly touched one, and their look had a new, breaking edge. ‘So these are where I’ll keep them.’

I swallowed. ‘I guess. Yes.’

‘Care to make a donation?’

I couldn’t refuse them. From this moment on, no-one ever could. My mouth spoke the ‘yes’ with brave adoration.

‘Of?’

‘Everything.’

They smiled a true smile and took my eyes from my sockets, my hands from my wrists and my heart from my ribcage and arranged them carefully, one to a spoke.

Part of me is still with them, living an unspeakably beautiful life.

The other part is here, giving you everything.

Angela L. Hicks

Bluebeard's Bride

They meet in Sofia—the Duke and the girl who will be his latest wife. He notices her serious, grey eyes watching him across a restaurant by the cathedral and sits down next to her.

They are married within the month. The Duke is not a patient man and he does not like to wait. The girl is an orphan; there is no one to object to the match. The Duke's acquaintances dare not interfere. They honeymoon in Italy and afterwards drive to the Duke's estate. It lies deep in the forests in eastern Bulgaria and the journey is long. As they travel, the girl asks her husband many questions about the area—how far they are from civilisation, how well sign-posted the way is—and listens closely to his answers. He delights in her curiosity. They are far from anywhere.

The Duke's castle is beautiful. His wife walks from room to room drinking in the opulence of the place; everything fascinates her. This pleases him; as they walk through the hundreds of rooms, each one filled with an unimaginable wealth of objects, he comments on the things he thinks interesting. He stops at a portrait.

'See the necklace the woman wears, isn't it beautiful? It's called the Heart of Ice and there isn't a diamond like it anywhere. It's a painting of my third wife; she loved diamonds.'

He waits for the inevitable question, but this new wife does not ask about her predecessors. She gazes at the picture.

'It's beautiful,' she agrees.

'I'll take you to see the diamond,' says the Duke. 'It's in the vaults along with all my other great treasures.'

The Duke's vaults are a wonder to behold, but there is something else down there; the passageway which leads to the vaults also leads to a small, black door studded with iron.

'That goes to the dungeons,' says the Duke, 'The door is locked. I've the key here on my ring, but you must never, ever open it.'

'I don't want to visit the dungeons,' says his bride. 'There'll be spiders and other nasty things.'

The Duke laughs. 'Yes, my other wives didn't much care for what was down there either.'

—

Several days later the Duke leaves his keys lying in their bedroom before he rides away on business. When he returns that evening they are gone. He questions his bride.

'I took them,' she admits, 'I fetched a bottle of wine from the cellar.'

'Is that the only door you unlocked?' asks the Duke, watching her closely.

The girl blushes. 'No.'

'Where else?' he cries.

'I also went into the vaults. I wanted to look at the Heart of Ice, wear it just for a few minutes.'

'You did not go into the dungeons?'

The girl shakes her head, and when the Duke later checks, he sees that the black door has not been unlocked. But he knows the weakness of women. In time…

Some weeks later the Duke goes away for several days. He leaves his wife his keys.

'Go anywhere you wish, my dear, apart from the dungeons. Never unlock that door,' he repeats.

When he returns, the Duke notices his wife watching him nervously at dinner. The room is dark—she has lit only a few candles—but he can sense her unease. He goes to the black door, but it has still not been opened.

'You did not go into the dungeons?' he asks.

'No, I have been exploring the house, redecorating and rearranging the rooms. I had no time to see the dungeons. Besides, you forbade me from entering them.'

The Duke frowns. He had thought he would be glad when at last he found a woman who could refrain from indulging in her curiosity, but now he discovers that this watching and waiting for her to fall to temptation is worse. The rest of the house no longer holds any joy for him. He does not approve of the changes his bride has made—it feels emptier now, colder, less filled with wondrous treasures—but he is too concerned with the locked door to chastise her about other matters. He lurks in the shadows, waiting for her to come, key in hand, to break her word to him.

But she never does. Sometimes she appears at the end of the passageway and he thinks that this is the moment, but she turns to the vault door instead and the Duke sits back with a sigh. Whether with relief or frustration, he is not certain.

He meets his wife in the entrance hall. She is dressed to go riding, furs wrapped up to her chin. She is bright-eyed; the Duke thinks her tense.

'You were on your way to the door, weren't you?' he crows.

'No. Look, your keys are there on the table, where you left them.'

He sees that she is right and snatches them up. When he turns around, she has gone, the front door swinging behind her. I am tired of waiting, he thinks, when she returns I will take her to the dungeons myself. Together we will unlock the door and go in.

He waits in their bedroom, gazing out of the window so that he will know the moment she rides home.

He waits for hours, until it is too dark for him to see the courtyard, or even the windowsill. He goes to light a candle. He cannot find the candelabra. There are no candlesticks in the passageway outside, nor in any of the other rooms. The rest of the silverware is also gone. So too the paintings and tapestries which until recently adorned the castle walls. He thinks of his bride's redecorating and wonders where she has put everything. He goes to the cellar: empty. The vaults: empty. Everything is gone.

Far away on the cathedral steps of Sofia, a girl shares a bottle of fine champagne with a companion. Her fingers play with the diamond at her throat. Heart of Ice.

Ashley Rauls

A Mutual Agreement

"Are you serious?" he asked, as we walked down the stairs of our apartment.

"Of course, I'm serious. When am I ever not serious about something? I followed through and moved to Brooklyn with you, remember?"

Brooklyn. Forever-dirty sidewalks that we walked daily. Liquor store that looked like it was broken into last night. Aspiring filmmaker trying to appear homeless with a Platinum American Express in back pocket. Rundown building with fence used to keep people out. Empty block. Michelin-starred restaurant. Casual. That's Brooklyn for you.

"You're serious." He nodded like he was listening to a political speech, trying to take in the main talking points. "I've never thought about it, I guess," he said, locking the main door. He took my hand and we headed down the sidewalk.

Never thought about it? He thought about everything. A scientist by trade after all. Scientists are taught to think about everything. Examine all possibilities.

"I haven't either, but it's just one of those things," I said. Me on the other hand. I was a screenwriter. Also trained to think of all possibilities.

"So you not only want a ring, but you also want a proposal?"

"Yes, and a proper one at that."

"How proper?"

"Down on one knee proper."

"God, you're killing me. Couldn't it be a mutual agreement?" he said, motioning to the coffee shop on our left.

I nodded.

The Beanery was our favorite because it had an ordering window. Quick, easy, and the coffee wasn't bad. The man in the window held up two fingers for two coffees, and we nodded.

"It would be mutual if you decide to propose and I decide to say yes."

Saying I wanted to marry him would have been an understatement. After meeting last autumn, I knew finding someone else wasn't an option. Sure, he was difficult at times. He's German, after all. The Germans aren't known for their flexibility. They're very matter of fact people, but I considered that a good thing. They know what they want. At least someone does in this world. And that told me that he would know what he wanted.

Me.

"Why do I have to be the one to propose?" he said, putting three dollars on the window ledge and picking up the cups. He handed the larger one to me and then reclaimed my free hand.

We continued on.

"What do you mean why do you have to be the one? If you want to marry someone, you propose to them."

"So why don't you propose to me?"

That was one thing I wasn't sure about, dating a German. Equal rights blah, blah, men and women are the same blah, gender equality blah, blah. Sure, you can judge, but sometimes I just want to be the woman a man opens the door for. The woman a man fights for. The woman a man...

"Because I want to be the woman a man proposed to." I drew his hand to my mouth and kissed the back of it. Repeating the motion, he overtook both of our hands, brought them to his mouth, and kissed the back of mine. "I'd say yes, if you were wondering," I added.

"But still...It's so traditional. So old."

"Your father proposed to your mother."

"Ah, sure he did, but that's the point. They're old. It's just an old tradition."

"It's one of those traditions I like."

"A big diamond?"

"It doesn't have to be big."

"But you'd be disappointed if it was small."

"It doesn't have to be big. When I'd say to others, *Yes, he proposed,* I don't want their jaws to drop, but I'd like them to respond with a *This is perfect* or *I'm happy for you.*"

"This overly expensive ring isn't the point. How practical is it?" He paused. Of course he brought up the P word. He's German after all. "You should have something durable. Would you wear this expensive ring every day? To the shops, to work, on holidays?"

"Of course. It's just a ring after all."

"Are you serious?"

"I moved to Brooklyn, didn't I?"

He tossed his coffee in the trash and stopped to roll a cigarette. We stood in front of Dean's Deli, the first meal we had the night we moved here. And now we were locals. Things can change in no time.

"Just a ring." He paused. Inhale. Exhale. "A ring that you spend a month's paycheck on. An entire month out of your life is gone. Just like that."

"Do you know how many months you live in one life?"

"Enough to know how much they're worth."

"Are you saying I'm not worth a month of your life?"

"You're worth a lifetime of months." And I believed him when he said that.

"It doesn't have to be a month. Two weeks. Hell, one week. A day. An hour of your life. For me."

Inhale. Exhale.

"Do I wear a ring as well?"

"You can if you'd like."

"A diamond one?"

"Well, that's not usually the case, but I suppose there could be diamonds."

"Wouldn't it be nice if our rings matched? Now that's a symbol."

"I like that idea. His and hers."

"But I don't want to buy my own ring. Where's the symbolism in that? Buy myself a ring to wear the rest of my life? I could do that without proposing."

"I could choose your ring."

Inhale. Exhale.

"But then it's not a surprise like yours. I don't get a surprise."

"Sometimes life is unfair, honey."

"I'm realizing that slowly but surely."

"It's not really about the surprise, though. It's about the thought. A person has thought and decided to ask another person to spend their lives together."

He finished the cigarette, stepping on what was left. Putting his arm around my waist, he pulled me closer.

"Ich liebe dich." I love you.

"Ich liebe dich, auch." I love you, too.

He's German, after all.

C.M.A. Hudson

Saplings

They only had one axe between them; it had been their father's. Jacob was bigger, though younger, so he took it. Malcolm stood beside him with his hands in his pockets.

"I imagine we ought to get started," said Jacob.

"Uh huh." Malcolm nodded. "Before we lose the sun."

"How we going to do it?"

Malcolm's jaw clicked as he thought. "Just get chopping, I suppose."

"You'll take over when I get tired?"

"You're pretty strong. You planning on getting tired?"

Jacob shrugged. "It's a big tree."

So it was. It was broad and sturdy, with a wide trunk and sonorous, wizened branches hanging all around.

"Might be we have to cut the boughs first," Malcolm said.

"That'll take hours."

"Take hours anyway."

"Why, with the boughs?"

Malcolm grunted. "It'll fall easier. And good for a warm-up."

Jacob held out the axe for his brother to take.

"I'm alright," Malcom told him.

"No, really. If it's a good warm-up, please, get cooking."

Malcolm didn't take the axe. He kept his hands stuffed into his pockets to keep the autumn wind from gnawing at them.

"Never looked at it much," Jacob said. "Must be real old. Older than both of us."

"Combined," Malcolm agreed. "Still an eyesore. That realtor said it'll force us to go in for a lower selling price."

Jacob grimaced. "He did." He swung the axe, like a batter on deck, to get a sense of its weight. "Might be worth the lower price."

"So the buyers can cut it down?"

"Fair enough."

"Jacob," Malcolm said. He turned to look at his brother. "It's better. That it's us. No crews, no machines."

Jacob nodded and gritted his teeth. "I know."

"I'll help you," Malcolm said. "When we get halfway, I'll help you. That's a promise."

Jacob didn't turn to look at Malcolm. He stared up at the tree their father had planted, long before either of them had been around. "It's a good tree," he told his brother.

"It is," said Malcolm.

They fell into silence for a time. A gust of wind danced by them, awash with little leaves.

"Alright," Jacob breathed. "Let's get started."

Neither moved.

Cecília Giannetti
That Day

"Surely you remember me?" she asked with tempting red lips as I waited for a taxi in the middle of a crowded street.

However, I didn't remember, which was very strange since I never forget a beautiful woman once I've seen one. It's a Darwinian photographic memory that we men have carefully developed along the centuries with the noble intention of identifying mates with good genes, and consequently saving us from the misfortune of having an ugly offspring.

Perhaps her décolletage was preventing me from thinking properly. I was feeling like a schoolboy unable to concentrate because his only pretty teacher decided to wear a short skirt while giving grammar lessons to some boys in puberty. Frankly, who cares about grammar when the study of anatomy is remarkably more didactic? Women should have more consideration for us easily distracted men. My spirit indeed was willing, but my flesh and memory were weak and I had no idea who she was.

"That day! Don't you remember?" she asked again, with a flirtatious smile.

Oh, God, that woman was killing me! "That day?" Was that all she could mention? Why could she not provide a slightly more specific indication of where we had met before, such as "that day at Elizabeth Crawford's birthday party in January last year, a snowy Saturday, at eight o'clock in the evening. I was wearing a voluptuous red dress and we discussed how muscular you looked in that new Christmas jumper your grandmother gave you." Nevertheless, she insisted on delivering enigmatic messages.

What could a man in my position possibly do?

"Of course I remember you! That day!" I said unblushingly.

"Yes! That day! I was sure you would remember," she sighed with relief.

This untimely lapse of memory raised the question of whether I should start taking medication for memory loss, or perhaps stop drinking.

No, medication was decidedly better.

"I don't remember if I got your number that day," the first clever thing I said. Exceedingly ingenious, actually. The considerable knowledge I had derived from reading Sherlock Holmes was finally useful, or perhaps from reading Playboy. I couldn't quite say which.

"Oh yes, I'm sure you have my number," she tenderly tapped me on the shoulder. Well, at least I'd tried. "Excuse me, I have to take this call," she said as her mobile began to ring. "Hello, this is Vanessa."

Vanessa! That was her name! I promptly started to make mental notes and tried to store her name in my long-term, no, eternal-term memory. I regarded this phone call not only as a most thoughtful intervention of Destiny, but also as an auspicious sign of the imminence of a passionate affair with Vanessa.

"Hi Rachel, how are you?" she continued her phone call, "I was just on my way home from work. You will not believe who I met! He's standing in front of me right now! No, not John. I haven't seen John again since we broke up."

I gazed at the sky and humbly thanked it for the fantastic news. John was no longer a hindrance to the success of my libidinous enterprise. And the phone call continued, "I'm here with Richard!"

Richard? I am no Richard. My name is Allan. A-L-L-A-N! I couldn't believe it. God generously presented me with the most perfect female specimen, only to discover her in the arms of a strange man called Richard. Many thanks, God. I'm sure Richard is a very nice guy indeed. He probably saves drowning children, plants many trees, brushes his teeth every night, even flosses them.

However, I could not afford to lose focus, for I was facing a crucial moment of decision. Would I follow the path of truth or the shortcut of lie? After careful consideration of the facts, I decided to embody Richard in order to prevent poor Vanessa from injuring her reputation and feeling embarrassed for seducing a complete stranger. Eventually, she hung up the phone.

"So, Vanessa, would you like to have some coffee?" I casually placed one hand on a shop window while the other hand sensually loosened my tie.

"Sure, Richard. There's a coffee shop just around the corner."

We sat strategically close to each other at the coffee shop, our yearning bodies almost touching. I was already in love. Her hair, her smile, her perfume... I simply loved the way she said my new name, Richard. Definitely, Richard was such a better name than Allan. I felt more handsome already.

"Tell me, Richard, how is Augustus doing?" she suddenly enquired.

"Augustus?" I asked. She started to laugh at my question and I started to sweat.

"Don't tell me you can't remember who he is!"

"Of course, I perfectly remember Augustus. I haven't seen him in a long time, but I guess he's just fine. He's a great guy," as I said those words, I wondered how I had become such a proficient liar. It was certainly a hunting instinct that males possess.

"What do you mean? Did you break up with Augustus? How terribly sad!

You were the sweetest couple I knew," her eyes expressed her sincere condolences as she gently pinched my cheek. Meanwhile, I sadly waved goodbye to my manliness as it walked away from the coffee shop.

Daniel Shand

All At Sea

We were huddled on the tilting deck, waiting to disembark—there were only a few lifeboats left and I was growing nervous. All the other men were standing back towards the ship's cabin, allowing the women and children to be helped first, the idiots. I was loitering behind the gaggle of little darlings, watching the coxswain as he selected candidates for the final lifeboat.

'You, you and you,' he said, pointing out a mother and her children. 'That's it. The rest of us will wait for the rescue boat.'

The crowd let out a groan, and the evil cloud continued to billow from our ship's funnel.

Fuck this, I thought, and barged through the children, moving their heads away with my hands.

'Hey,' shouted the coxswain, but I was already making my way down the rope ladder, having elbowed the lucky woman and her children to the side.

The lifeboat was tiny, but it would suit my needs. I balled up the rain cover and threw it into the ocean. To my horror, there was a boy curled up between the benches.

'Seth,' the lucky woman shouted from above me, descending the ladder.

I kicked against the side of the ship and sat down to row in earnest. The boy crawled to the prow to hold his hand out towards his mother as we moved away from her. He must have smuggled himself aboard without me noticing. That was hardly my fault, was it?

'It's no use pal,' I told him. 'I'm rescuing us.'

He bawled all through that first night. 'You're just dehydrating yourself,' I told him, but he took no notice.

We watched the sunrise together. It sulked up from the horizon, bleeding its flower colours into the sky and the sea. There was nothing to disturb the waves anywhere around us.

'That's some sight, eh Seth? Not many men get the chance to see a sight as fine as that.'

The ungrateful pig didn't acknowledge me, just sulked in the little den he'd made inside the prow.

He considered me with flat eyes. 'Where's my mother?'

'Suit yourself,' I told him.

I awoke hours later to find my mouth gummed shut from sleep and the sea air. Sitting up, I realised the boy was missing. I checked under the filthy blanket he'd brought along. Nothing.

There was, however, a small black spot bobbing a hundred yards or so out in the water. I rowed towards it.

'You're a fine swimmer,' I said when I reached him.

I wasn't being honest. He was struggling to keep himself above water, spitting and heaving for air. I pulled him aboard by the scruff of his shirt and deposited him in a sodden lump. He called me a foul name and I had to stifle my laughter.

'What did you want me to do Seth? Let you drown?'

He wrung some ocean out of his trousers and said, 'Yes.'

I won't deny that the first day or two was difficult. There was a voice in my head reminding me that a person can only go three days without water. Once or twice I attempted to snatch a fish from the school that trailed our boat but they were too quick for me. Was it the case that you could catch things like seabirds and turtles and drink the liquid from their insides? I couldn't remember, but it didn't matter anyway. Seth and I had little chance of catching ourselves a turtle.

We lost the light that evening and decided to bed down for the night. 'What's the first thing you're going to do when you get home?' I asked Seth.

'Find my father.'

'That's a good one. I wouldn't mind tracking down some of my old pals either. It's funny how times like these make you sentimental, isn't it Seth? But no. It's going to be milk for me. A chilled bottle of fresh milk with the cream thick on top. Oh yes.'

Seth turned away from me to face into the prow. I was worried about how the desiccated skin on his lips was beginning to flake away. For all of his impertinence, I was growing fond of the boy. I'd never had a son of my own, and I suppose during the days we were at sea I started to consider the prospect as something desirable.

On the third day the gods smiled down upon the two of us. As I was rowing, Seth cried out in joy. I turned to see a dark smear of land on the edge of the horizon. Redoubling my efforts, I managed to get us there in no time. Seth spoiled the mood somewhat by crouching at the edge of the boat, waiting to spring free as soon as we hit land.

And that was exactly what he did. The boat lurched as I banked it on the sand and Seth threw himself onto the beach and began sprinting. I started after him but I needn't have bothered. He didn't get far.

A crowd of natives emerged from the trees at the head of the beach and stopped him in his tracks. The brute I took to be the chief carried the boy across the sand towards me. He was a huge person, the chief, and wore a garland of clustered berries. The rest of what I suppose was his tribe waited at the treeline, brandishing spears and shields.

I wiped my mouth as the chief approached. He had a good foot of height on me. He tossed Seth onto the beach at my feet. The boy struggled but the chief put his bare sole across his back and eyed me up.

He said, 'Your son.'

'Yes,' I said. 'Thank you.'

The chief nodded and then his face broke into a wide grin. He put his hand on my neck. 'Come,' he said.

Eben Diskin

The Honeymoon Suite

[excerpt from a longer work]

Richard Roswell was considering how marriage is nothing more than a bad restaurant. You order one thing and get another, or what you ordered comes undercooked or full of grease, and unless you want to make a scene, at the end you still have to pay the bill.

The decision to end the marriage was mutual, meaning it was all her idea. For nine years he had Isabel. For nine generally pleasant years Roswell had enjoyed the same restaurant, only to watch the food slowly expire, and one day, inexplicably, he was turned away at the door. All he could do was remember. A professional would have advised against that, but real professionals were difficult to come by, as he would soon learn. For the time being his thoughts remained perversely focused, conjuring sad reminiscences.

A building came into his head, twenty stories tall, stately as a gray politician. His brain in a haze, his feet dragged him to the doorstep of the Hotel Charlatan, where he had first won Isabel's affections over wine and duck.

It was an elegant place with hardwood floors and chandeliers, and paintings of anonymous men on the lobby walls. These features struck Roswell like the sight of an old friend, but one who'd decayed and become hollow. In the restaurant candles were still on every table, and the grandfather clock that signaled the hour was still in the corner. It was seven.

"What is the matter with me?" he thought after taking a seat. "Why come here? Why sit at this table, of all tables, where we shared our first meal? This was my chair and that was her chair. The tablecloth is the same. I wonder if it's the same candle, which made her face glow orange."

They were out of duck so he settled for wine. After the second glass he realized how foolish he was for even considering food. Duck confit had never helped anyone forget their troubles. He ordered a third glass, then a fourth, and in an hour he had lost count, for his mind was in a cloud.

He scratched his signature on the bill and, quite by accident, left the waitress a three-hundred and ten dollar tip. The number was in his head. 310. Stumbling to the elevator, he pressed the button for the third floor.

Room 310 overlooked Abingdon Square Park. He stayed there with Isabel on their first weekend away together, which he'd begun planning the moment she expressed how much she adored the grandfather clock in the corner. "It's enchanting," she had said. "Like the rest of this place. Old, but a good old."

He admired the clock too, which was not surprising because they loved many of the same things. He listed them in his head as he went down the hallway, leaning on the wall for support.

"Antiques, golf, whiskey, people watching, chocolate, white chocolate, chocolate with nuts, wintertime, Jacuzzis in the wintertime..."

Room 310 was locked. No answer came from knocking, and he recalled vividly the view of the park from the room's balcony. A bronze statue of a soldier marked the middle, and from there cobblestones wove through the park and gardens. It had been a spring evening. He and Isabel relaxed on the balcony, and for the first time all season the wind was not frigid, but warm.

"Isabel!" he called, imagining that she was on the balcony without him. "Isabel!"

He slogged back to the elevator. When it opened he fumbled with the buttons and fell to the ground in tears. Frankie Lymon & the Teenagers was playing on the sound system, singing a familiar tune from the 50s. It filled Roswell with a vague nostalgia.

The elevator halted abruptly, with a jolt. The lights overhead began to flicker, then went black.

The wine had made him restless. He returned the gun to his coat and paced the confined space as if that could somehow revive the broken mechanisms. As he did he heard a muffled sound, not of whirring machinery but of humanity. It was voices, loudest by the back wall of the elevator. He ran his hands along its wood surface and found a handle, which must have functioned as a door slide for service personnel. With some effort he pushed it aside, revealing a doorway embedded in the side of the elevator shaft across the way. A false step would mean a plummet of at least ninety feet, but he thought nothing of the fall.

Carelessly he crossed the gap and went through the door. A few steps brought him to a corridor smelling of dampened wood, and it peeled under his feet. It was much like the other halls filled with guests, but this one was abandoned; not cleaned in a decade from the looks of it. The wall-mirrors were caked with dust. One room was situated in the center, marked by the bronze number "400." If not for the light underneath this door, the hall would have been completely black. Now, he perceived the voices clearly. He knocked softly, again and again, to no reply. At last he took the knob.

No less than twenty men were smoking cigars in a space that looked more like a private study than a hotel room. There was a fireplace between two bookcases, a bar at one end and a billiards table at the other. The blackwood walls made the room dim, and the air seemed crisp, though filled with cigar smoke. It felt like coming home to a bright hearth after a long trek in the cold.

"Who is that?" asked one man, taking a puff.

"I don't know," said another. "Did you invite him?"

A silver-haired fellow shook his head. "Never seen him in my life. What is your name?"

"Richard Roswell," the divorcee replied after a moment. "What—"

"Roswell?" the silver-haired man interrupted. "I don't recognize that name. Is he on the list?"

A younger man sitting in the corner rose from his seat and flipped through a black notebook on the bureau.

"He is not a candidate."

The silver-haired man took the cigar out of his mouth and approached Richard, inspecting him as he would a racehorse.

"Well, I don't know who he is, but he looks glum. Bitter. Depressed. He must have come here on purpose."

Florence Vincent

Tokens

Sometimes her eyes go dead when I'm lying on top of her, and I wonder if she's thinking of him. It's subtle. A slight turn of the head, a slackening in her features and the strange sense that even though she's right there beneath me, held tight between the mattress and my body, she's somehow fallen away. Gone to a place I'm not welcome.

Inevitably, even after I've rolled off her or brought her back to me by squeezing her tummy and making her giggle, I can't help but go back to the sight of her standing in the hallway that day. Me hearing the front door close but no sound back when I say hello, so I walk from the kitchen – there's stir fry burning on the hob, I think – to find Kate stood there, face dead white, blood all over her. It's on her tights and her dress but mainly splashed across her pale grey jacket, against which the red patches look beautifully vivid.

The really annoying thing is, I can't remember if her eyes used to do that before it happened. Maybe they always did. Maybe it's not that they're going dead at all but that she's taken over with pleasure, or sleepiness, or thinking about those bitches at work (the worst being Molly, whose head I'd happily smash in even though sometimes I think of her body when I'm fucking Kate). Maybe it's just me, looking for something in her.

I pull my arm gently from underneath her neck and sit up enough to look down on her sleeping. There's a wedge of creamy light coming in the door (she doesn't like complete darkness) and it's illuminating her, lying on her side, knees tucked up, hands under her cheek as though she's a statue in a churchyard. I've often wondered how she sleeps like that, so perfectly still.

When I'm certain she's out for the count I get up and go over to the cupboard, opening it with one hand, pressing the other to the hinges to stop it from creaking. The jacket hangs at the end, zipped up in one of those plastic suit covers, tucked away out of sight behind my winter coats. I slip it out, folding it over my arm, and move out of the bedroom, pressing my feet softly on the carpet, carefully avoiding the places where the floorboards squeak.

In the spare room, I sit on the edge of the bed and unzip the cover, letting it fall to the ground like a dress slipping off a woman's body. The jacket is slightly warm from the water pipes in the wall next to the cupboard and the effect is unearthly, as though it has recently been worn. I lay it on my lap, running my hands gently over it, concentrating on the patterns of red, remembering.

She sat on the edge of the bath as it filled, swallowing hard over and over, as though there was a lump of something in her throat. I wiped at her hands with a wet flannel and then took the jacket off her, laying it carefully over the towel rail. Then I pulled her dress up over her head and peeled down her tights. The blood had soaked through to her bra and was browning in little spots.

Get rid of it, she said, looking at the pile of clothes.

Get rid of what?

All that. The jacket. Everything.

I'll get it cleaned.

No, get rid of it. Get rid of it. Please get rid of it.

I looked back at her, eyes so wide and wet, and nodded.

The jacket is expensive. Hip-length, a pale blueish grey. The fabric is slightly silky but there's a stiffness to the arms that indicates it's barely been worn. Afterwards, I went out and bought her a new suit, an expensive one with lilac silk lining. She's worn it so much it's started to go shiny from being dry-cleaned too often. She doesn't know that I've ordered her a new one for her birthday – narrow grey pinstripe, pencil skirt.

Another thing Kate doesn't know: the morning after it happened I crept downstairs, turned over her boots and found, tucked away into one of the soles, a small white token. I prised it out and held it up to the light. The tooth had broken clean – no blood – and I wondered at the likelihood of me finding such a thing. It's about knowing where to look, I suppose. The girl who had thrown herself from the top of the library in second year, her teeth spreading beautifully in a wide arc like a sprinkling of snow, had been my introduction to all this. And to think, I had just happened to be passing when she jumped. The luck of it.

The man who jumped from Kate's office block was called Jay. He was twenty-one and in his Facebook profile picture he's holding a pint and has his arm draped casually around a friend. No one knows why he did it, just as no one knows that if you were to reach into the unused left football boot stuffed at the back of my wardrobe, you would find a prescription pill bottle, empty now save for two small shards of tooth. One of his, one of hers.

Outside, a fox shrieks and my head jolts back. I realize how tightly I'm holding the jacket, find that my whole body is tensed. I stand and open the window, allow a little breeze in, my skin tingling from the excitement of just holding the thing. Back in the bedroom, I slip the jacket quietly into the wardrobe and it's only when I'm getting into bed that she stirs, eyebrows creasing, small anxious whimper falling from her lips. I nestle against her, wrap an arm around her body, put my mouth close to her ear.

I've got you, I whisper, hugging her tight. *I've got you.*

Gwydion Roberts

Transgender Journal: The Wolf's Lair

[excerpt from a longer work]

I've never explored it, Hitler's Wolf's Lair, warned like all local children not to go in there, the forest with its unexploded land mines and millions of mosquitoes. I've wandered into that forest only in dreams, the last with autumn colours and the leaves divested to find the concrete husks of a place where one of history's darkest tyrants grew more frantically murderous with his victims, while casting his own people in an ever more sacrificial light. To wander that forest even in dreams will not give you the contemplative peace such places are meant for. In my dream it turned into a castle of skulls in a forest without birds or greenery, no life at all until the dream faded into something else again.

My eyes gaze at the forest from my apartment as afternoon is turning to dusk. I light a cigarette at the backdoor and exhale. In this dusk I watch a man in black grow smaller until the forest takes him into its darkness. I finish the cigarette and close the backdoor with a thud in the silence and everything becomes darker as my eyes adjust. I have a film to watch, about monsters that come alive in the light of the moon.

I stride across to the kitchen in my three-inch heels and pour myself a glass of red wine, flinching inwardly at the sound I make on the tiles. What will the neighbours make of it? They know me as a single man in his twenties. Are they putting their ears to the walls like the staff of Doctor Jekyll, wondering what's become of me?

The following morning.

I stand at the backdoor and become aware that a neighbour too is smoking at her backdoor. In my new zest I had transformed in daylight into a skirt and top, savouring the morning and my smooth skin when I am least what I dislike about myself, but as a result I cannot stand in the sunlight. If I stand there she sees me, the breeze blowing my long skirt into the open. I wonder if she's watching, my smoke exhaled, the distended arm and the hand holding the cigarette, smoke emerging from a pair of lips but nothing more. Does she think me agoraphobic? A person scared of daylight. Or perhaps she saw enough of the skirt as it blew through the door and she knows the truth. I hope I avoid her on a future walk, her and her pushchair on the way to a nursery perhaps, to tell her friends of the freak next door.

Another morning.

Another cigarette, having checked to see that the neighbour's not there. As I smoke, I see on the tree above me a collared dove who's looking for the cat. If the cat comes, the birds fly away. If I see a neighbour, I retreat into the darkness of my apartment and I'm not too dissimilar to the bird in this respect though they have the sky to fly to, while I have just this apartment.

Apartment, a perfect name for this place I inhabit, cut off from others, alone in a self-imposed exile for this appearance I've chosen, though in truth and because of the sadness that overwhelms me otherwise, it's not much of a choice.

Another Saturday.

No monster film for me. There is only one place of monsters left and I know where that exists. My apartment is empty, dark, my make-up and a change of clothes packed and taken with me. The neighbours have their barbecues, their laughter, it carries on the breeze.

A breeze that penetrates this summer forest, where the slim branchless linden trees stand among the thicker, more muscular oaks, and the green ground is interspersed with the purple of the Siberian Iris and the Globeflower's yellow.

It is evening as the man in black walks towards the forest. Within the forest am I, changing, with silver talons and large eyes to see him better with and lips as red as blood. And as my true form completes its transformation, I see the man between the trunks and boughs walk by. It's dark enough that he doesn't see me, dark enough for me to follow his trail with the scent of his aftershave, some kind of musk from a well-known deodorant, until he's at the concrete husks and he pulls out his cigarette, waiting. He is not alone, I sense the shadows of others, watching me as I stalk towards him.

He hears my footsteps. In long suede boots of black I approach, trampling twigs and grass underneath to see him smile as I come towards him, until I'm inches from him. He could beat me now, leaving me for dead and the world need never know or care, but he tells me I'm beautiful. "Prove it," I say without thinking, and his hands go to my neck then to my cheeks, he caresses me and we kiss, and he proves it.

He takes me by the hand to a slab of mossy concrete in the moonlight, and during this night we will be what we are in the forest amid the wildlife and the husks of a bunker built by a man who failed to wipe out people like ourselves. And now I believe that to want to exist is not monstrous, but to stop others from doing so might be, and perhaps there are no such things as monsters, just actions, like this man's caresses and the heartbeat he affects in me.

But in the dawn I walk back alone from the forest and the Wolf's Lair, a place of stolen moments in the moonlight that still feels like an underworld. Here I am, always wanting more. When you exist in a cage you always want more, you want the sky, the whole damn thing. And I'm left wondering, was this freedom or just a cage made larger?

Ignacio B. Peña

The Ghost

The doorbell rings twice and Mark gets up after a pounding on the door and that makes that what? The eleventh time tonight? They're coming thick and fast now. What this time, spray-painted potato sacks? Maybe a gaggle of lonely witches shivering in the night looking for somewhere to warm up.

Hang on, these are kids man, not some seedy Halloween office dive. Jesus.

Mark takes the bowl of fun-size snickers and candy corn because fuck that, only my little girl gets the peanut butter cups, not you you little shits. He opens the door and they blast him with a full force HAPPY HALLOWEEN screaming into his ears.

Two little goblins, a green frumpy witch. Little-boy Spiderman. A short woman grinning at her brood, the charming things. The little monsters stretch out their arms holding their plastic jack-o-lanterns and bags, probably big stupid grins under those ugly masks of theirs, ready for their treat. Mark scoops one thick hand into the bowl and, from left to right, drops one-two-three-four pieces of candy. Stops on a fifth. A lanky teenage boy in a hoodie stands next to little Spiderman, holding a plastic shopping bag. Just a gray fucking hoodie and jeans, sad little mustache.

Mark withdraws the candy in his hand and drops it back into his bowl, looks at the teenager and says no.

"No? Dude, how you gonna do me like that?"

"You're not even tryin man. No." Mark looks to the woman. She's about to open her mouth but he tightens the bowl to his chest and smiles wide. No. Fucking. Way.

The kids are pulled off the porch lightly by the shoulders. The woman bends down to the little witch and shoots a side glance back to Mark, tells the children in a flat tone to say thank you to the nice man and her brood yell THANK YOU NICE MAN as they walk away. The teenager slinks behind, shoots up his arm, middle finger raised high at the porch, a silent fuck you nice man.

Mark shuts the door and locks it, dropping the bowl onto the side table.

Gray hoodie and jeans, fuck you kid.

His back pocket chimes and he pulls out his phone. Text from Pepper. She gets the peanut butter cups, you little shits. A photo of a little girl draped in a white sheet with her arms spread wide out, with a note underneath.

Look daddy, I'm a ghost!

Mark stares at the little ghost on his phone for a long while before he looks up to the photo on the wall of him and Pepper and Beth sitting on a blanket out on Progress Park. She hates this photo. Won't shut up how it's the only time we ever went. Couldn't even give me fuckin Halloween though. She hates Halloween, at least just give me the girl on Halloween.

Another text. Beth.

Dammit.

Next time she's over, make sure there's some goddamn milk.

The doorbell rings.

Mark doesn't move, he just stares at the photo, at the blanket on the grass, the light pouring onto golden wisps of Pepper's hair, on Beth's face, her smile. Her silver-blue eyes.

How do I get back to that?

The doorbell rings one-two-three and there's pounding on the door and goblins and witches and all sorts of vile creatures in the night squeal trick or treat outside. Mark walks away to the hall, grabs a pair of scissors, opens the linen cabinet.

Outside the group of trick-or-treaters are turning to walk away from the porch when the front door opens. The kids in costume turn around excited and begin to yell trick but stop before treat. A tall ghost has opened the door, steps out onto the porch and closes the door behind him. Two eyes peer out at them from cut holes in a long white sheet.

No parents.

He reaches into the bag of a tiny mummy and pulls out a snickers bar and throws it out onto the lawn. Then he reaches into the bag of the pirate girl next to him and does the same thing to a handful of jolly ranchers. The group of kids turn around screaming, running into the street.

The ghost walks toward the footpath in a slow, measured pace and turns right. Groups of children, little demons and things, scatter around the sheeted wraith as he walks upright past them, paying them no mind. Parents hold their children close. Some let loose a nervous little laugh into the dark. He stands at driveways, staring at groups of kids yelling at doors for their candy. When they turn around and leave those porches they start and scream when they see the ghost staring at them. They stare back, frozen, until the ghost moves on from there satisfied, as if he's delivered them a glimpse of their days to come.

The ghost walks into the convenience store around the corner and reaches in the dairy section for a gallon of milk and for a box of lucky charms. He walks up to the counter and sets down the milk and the cereal, saying nothing. The clerk eyes him a moment before ringing him up.

"Five eighty."

The ghost places six single dollar bills before the clerk. The clerk doesn't take the money, he just stares at the man in the sheet before him.

"It's not quite the same, is it?" he asks.

A sigh from underneath the sheet.

"No. I guess it's not."

The ghost walks back to his empty porch, sparsely lit within the hungry darkness. He stops at the top step and hovers over the pumpkin his daughter carved yesterday before Beth took her from him again. He lifts his foot and rests it on top of the jack-o-lantern, pressing down his weight until the orange skin cracks and splits and caves in on the candle flickering inside.

Jt Fels

Hell or High Roller

[excerpt from a longer work]

I.

“Two entries left. Are you ready, Mister Schaefer?”

I nodded my head and followed the figure through the door.

Porcelain bones and black suit. Was it ever human? I asked myself, trailing behind the figure. Like a high-end Halloween fixture, it seemed too flawless, too polished. Each passing light reflected off the back of the perfect skull, eager to burn its place into your memory.

It seemed everything around me wished to brand my senses. The blackened walls smelled of cheap liquor. Ashes floated through the air like common dust. You could not open your mouth without tasting it; the remnants of whatever may have been.

“You are progressing quicker than most, Mister Schaefer.”

Around the corner, the playful screams of children. A little girl and boy came into view, the girl’s Shirley Temple curls brushing against the figure’s black suit as they ran past us.

“Such a shame, the little ones.” It never turned its head toward me. “They often accrue the least debt. Little theft, maybe a handful of lies. Very rarely, will you find one with blood on their hands. And yet, they fill the river more than their elders. If only they knew to make better use of their time.” It stalled for a moment at the split in the corridor. “Were you a father, Mister Schaefer?”

“No.”

“Ah,” the figure began again, turning the corner, toward the doorway. “A blessed life, perhaps. Our more parental guests tend to have a harder time when visiting the Scene.”

Each footstep soaked into the frayed carpet. Their muffled echoes failed to make it down the corridor. Distant piano and quiet croons of diluted lounge music seeped through the doors ahead leading to the playing floor. Behind us, I could hear the children running back down the hallway, screaming and laughing. I envied their ignorance.

The figure stopped at the door and pulled out its pocket watch.

“Oh, dear,” it said, opening the door enough to look inside. “We will need to be more punctual tomorrow if you are to join them. Can’t have you late to your final outing, can we, Mister Schaefer? Now, if you would be so kind as to present your arm—"

I pushed the sleeve up on my right arm. Eleven burns along the underside of my arm.

"Thank you, Mister Schaefer," it said, handing me the match.

I pressed the match against my skin and allowed the flame to seep through the blistering flesh on my wrist; my rite of passage. I knew I wouldn't feel it until I next awoke but when I did, it would hurt. God dammit, would it hurt. I relinquished the match to the figure's skeletal hand. The flame extinguished upon contact.

"Your chips have been relocated to locker 3433 in preparation of tomorrow's potential festivities." It handed me the key. "Good luck and high fortunes."

II.

Twelve thousand, eight hundred hands at the main table, from open to close, reserved for the men on their final entry. Until the last hand is dealt, we'd play, hoping for the highs to be with us. It helped to not focus on the number of chips remaining. On the twelfth day, however, the bag feels heavy to everyone and doubt dangles above our heads; we may never empty our bags.

The King and his Eight, The Soft Ace with a Jack, Tens of Spades and Hearts. These were my trophies; the moments when I saw the dealer remove my chips from the table. They were silent creatures. Genderless corpses, stripped of any distinguishing feature from one another. At each table, they stood, quietly handing our fates to chance, amidst the waves of desperation, waiting for our hit or stay.

Facing the Queen on the table, I looked to my hand. Nine and Eight.

"Stay."

The Queen is joined by another. My chips are doubled and returned to me. It was the same rush of anger as every loss before. Each time, it consumed a little more of me. The weight of a crime, like a casino token, means little on its own. But as we accrue them, the burden increases. Stack anything high enough and it crashes back down, scattering the pieces about—some we are bound to forget. I have the misfortune of having found my crimes; to see them in their numbers.

I wasn't going to beat this.

"Let us see what your earnings were today, shall we, Mister Schaefer?" It emptied the bag into the dark red machine behind the counter. "Not to worry; there's always tomorrow, my friend. Plus forty chips for a total of one hundred, eighty-seven chips."

One hundred, eighty-seven chips, a life's worth of lying; of cheating and greed. I hated that bag; how full it always seemed, how heavy it was at the end of each entry. Everything I did. Everything I owe.

"Now, now, Mister Schaefer; don't look so distraught. Tomorrow, you play at the main table; you may bet as much as you wish." It hands me the key to locker 3433. "There will be medication administered to your room. It will help to suppress the Scene, if you so wish."

III.

The Scene, they called it. You live it and relive it, yet no one sees it the same. The screams of the passengers, shattering glass, the force of pushing against the brake pedal, the brakes not being enough. Never gets easier. Twelve times and it was never easier. Each time, I felt the glass in my fingertips, bone scraping against bone. Each time, I heard the silence, followed by distant sirens that never make it in time. I'd see it again and again, Angie's lifeless stare; her last sight of the cheat she remained so blissfully unaware of. Can you see me? I'd ask her; the only words I could say. You learn to cope with the sight but soon it becomes the only way you remember someone; the way they look when the blood stops flowing.

Kelly Pierce

Class Clown

She never laughed. She never reacted, and that was even worse than the girls that groaned. I always had shit to say in Spanish class and even though my shit was so damn predictable, at least half the class still got a kick out of it. Even Señora had to bite her lip to hold her head steady. But this one chick—she never laughed. At the beginning of the semester, I didn't know her; I didn't even know her name. But I obsessed like a stalker. She got her hair cut about every six weeks; trimmed her bangs back above her eyebrows. When her hair was long enough that she could braid it down her shoulder, you knew it was time for the cut. She wore the same brand of jeans every day; those ones with the yellow stripe stitched diagonally down each back pocket. I think purple was her favorite color because she always wore purple sneakers and purple eye shadow, but never purple shirts, which was strange. Her shirts were plain—light grey, heather grey, dark grey, brown, or black, and no logos or designs. She drove a navy 2008 Acura TL and she got to class five minutes before the bell. She was always so serious, like some sort of battle was going on in her brain that distracted her from the outside world—and my clever one-liners. Come on, girl. Take a load off. I wanted her to laugh. I wanted to make her laugh.

It was one of those days when Señora gave us a worksheet and, since we were all about to graduate, the class just goofed around as Señora paced the classroom. My buddies and I didn't stop goofing when she walked by us. I was throwing around my normal morning banter loud enough for the girl to hear—just total garbage about how learning the conjugations of the imperfect won't get me anywhere in the Dominican Republic when I'm looking for the nearest casino. That got a few chuckles from my usual fans, including Señora, of course.

In an attempt to keep up with the times, Señora went, "Are you boys going to prom?" My buddies grunted and, I shit you not, I came out with this response: "Señora, I'm not going to prom unless I'm guaranteed pussy."

The girl had stopped writing and she turned her cheek, just so one of her eyes was on me. I couldn't read her expression but it was the first time I had ever seen her brown eye locked on mine. I felt my armpits dampen. Then Señora, trying too hard to be cool, leaned over to the girl and her friends and said, "Well it's never guaranteed! Am I right, ladies?"

The girl shrugged. "I'm not going either," she said, pulling a piece of her hair around her finger and moving her eye back to the worksheet. Now my armpits were fucking soaked.

"Oh, no! Why isn't anyone going to prom?" Señora cried in despair.

"I'm going!" called out the chunky girl across the room who thought she was more interesting than she was. And then everyone else started chiming in about prom and I tuned it out. I didn't care. I just kept staring at her hunched spine in that heather grey shirt.

The bell rang and she didn't take a fucking breath before she was out of her seat. I blinked and she was gone. I grabbed my backpack, still open, papers flying out of it and I ran down the hall after her.

"Hey," I shouted. "HEY," I shouted again, so everyone around me looked at me like I was doing something important. She turned around and her face looked a way I'd never seen before. It was confusion, yeah, confusion. Her right eye twitched and her lip was curled.

I was kind of panting at this point—too many cigarettes and too much weed fucking with my lungs. So between breaths I asked, "Do you want—to go—to Prom—with me?"

Her face was blank and then it kind of just exploded. She was laughing so hard that spit sprayed onto my face. Tears were forming in her eyes, she nearly fell to the floor she was laughing so hard. At first, I was elated, thinking she and I were sharing some sort of moment.

And then she said, "No! Hell no!" She had to catch her breath; "No *way* will I go to Prom with you!" She turned around and walked away, her laughter reverberating off the lockers.

Lori Sheirich

My Mother Always Said

Inspired by Edwin Morgan's poem
'Glasgow 5 March 1971' (With a ragged diamond)

My mother always said that loving him would be the death of me. That if I wasn't careful, he would pull me into the back alleys and side streets of his life, the darkness of his not-quite-legal ways. But to know Deacon was to love him—the sharp quickness of his tongue, the gleam in his eye. He was an ice-cold drink on a summer day. And for me, to know him was to never want to let him go.

When his phone calls first tapered off and it was heard around town that he'd taken up with a girl named Annabelle, a girl as fast and street-wise as him, I walked with my back straight and my head held high. Only my mother knew that the pillows were wet at night when I finally succumbed to sleep.

'You're better off without him,' friends would tell me.

'He doesn't deserve you,' family would agree.

I nodded dumbly no matter what was said. It made no difference. They didn't know him the way I did. But on the day I heard Annabelle was pregnant and they had set a date to marry, I knew it was time to make some changes of my own. I began to go through the nursing school acceptance letters that had been sitting on my desk for weeks. The type of program each offered no longer mattered, only the location was important. The university farthest from Glasgow would be the place I would start my new life.

News must have traveled to Deacon, because the day before I left he called and said he needed to see me one more time; there were things left unsaid and he wanted to make it right. I knew things could never be the same between us, but there's nothing so tempting as the possibility of hearing something you've desperately longed for. I agreed to meet him on my way to Central Station to catch my train.

I got up especially early the morning I was leaving, wanting to take my time to get ready. I fixed my hair the way I knew he preferred it and put on my favourite dress. I wrapped myself in my brand-new slick white raincoat, a gift from my mother, and carefully applied my trademark shade of lipstick—a soft and subtle pink. Deacon was waiting for me as I got off the bus.

'Hello, Liz,' his voice cracked. He had a small bouquet of wildflowers in his left hand which he extended to me. 'Peace offering,' he mumbled, not quite meeting my eyes.

'They're lovely,' I admitted, and they were—a profusion of pink, lavender, and white flowers that looked both delicate and resilient. 'Shall we head to the train station for a coffee? My train is at half past eleven, so that gives us a little time to chat.'

He looked up as though surprised by my suggestion. 'I thought we could go to that coffee shop we both used to like so much. The one with the red door on Sauchiehall Street. Just for old times' sake.'

By agreeing to go to the coffee shop he suggested, I knew I would miss my train and it would be a few hours before the next one would arrive. But that was ok. No one would be the wiser. And so we set off, making our way slowly towards the coffee shop, stopping to admire window displays just like we had in the past. The comfortable familiarity of him by my side came rushing back.

A few doors away from our destination, two of Deacon's former friends, Tommy and Ross, appeared across the street. Growing up, the three of them had been inseparable; never did you see two of them without the third. As children they had been daredevils and as they grew so did the boldness of their escapades. When Tommy and Ross were caught breaking into a store while Deacon managed to get away, they served their time without complaint. But since then things had never been the same. Both Tommy and Ross had made it clear that they believed Deacon had yet to repay his debt to them. I saw them before Deacon did and grabbed his arm as they began to swiftly move towards us.

'Deacon, let's get out of here,' I managed, trying to pull him forward. But rather than move with me, Deacon turned to face them. Suddenly, Tommy and Ross were in front of us. And as though a conductor ordered it, life began to move in half time as I watched Deacon fall backwards at Tommy's push. Deacon's arms starfished out as he fought to regain balance. His right hand grabbed my coat, but the backward momentum was too much for me to fight and I soon felt myself tipping backwards as well. I could hear my own scream intermingle with the tinkling sound of shattering glass as our heads hit the shop window behind us. The icicles of plate glass began to rain down on us tentative at first, then faster and harder. I watched as red poppies began to bloom along the bottom of my coat and across its sleeves. I turned my head towards Deacon. His beautiful face bristled with shards of glass. I looked above me and watched as another piece of plate glass fell, ripping through the collar of my coat. I could feel the warmth of blood seeping down my arms, my face, my neck. I laid my head back as it continued to rain.

Madelyn Harris

Blue Ceramic Mugs

Today was the day that I had been dreaming of and the day that simultaneously made me feel like I could vomit any time between now and the downbeat of the overture for the opening night of my show. Leaving my apartment complex, I stepped from the welcoming warmth of the lobby into the bitter cold. A gush of wind surprised me, hitting me with a punch. I took a second to regain my breath. Usually the wind was a friend that pushed and guided me to my destination. But today, it was harsh. It cut like a razor.

I pulled my jacket closer around me, checking my watch before tucking my hands under my armpits. Seventeen minutes until call time. I would get there on time, but just barely.

Thoughts ran through my head at lightning speed. I hoped I had remembered to put my costume in my dressing room. Did the set designers finish painting the backdrop? Jeff always forgot his line; he better not forget it tonight. The after party! I forgot to bring a dish for the after party!

I rounded the corner of Highland Avenue, walking briskly past a pop-up coffee vendor that I had never seen before. The man from behind the register called out to me.

"Good morning, miss. Care for a cuppa coffee?"

I picked up my pace, shaking my head. "No thanks," I said quietly, glancing at my watch again. No pit stops allowed this morning.

Feeling a strong gust of wind, I inhaled the rich scent of coffee grains. It smelled strangely familiar. I stood in the way of the wind and let the fragrance hit me again. The realization came to me; the smell was reminiscent of my grandma's house. Whether winter or summer, there was always a pan of coffee beans roasting on the stovetop that made her entire house smell like java. Grandma's coffee was one-of-a-kind; she bought her beans from some off-beaten hippy store downtown and added her own secret flavors while they roasted. Her coffee had a distinct smell and taste: mildly acidic, revealing traces of blackcurrant tartness, though also possessing a strong caramel sweetness. It was an odd amalgamation of flavors, one that could not be easily duplicated.

And yet, this was the same exact smell. It stopped me dead in my tracks.

My eyelids closed, and I practically felt Grandma's soft hands stroking my hair as we sat on her porch swing, which creaked slightly every time it rocked.

I pictured the way her soft hazel eyes looked into mine, the way she let me lay my head onto her lap as I sobbed and sniffled, covering her skirts in mascara smears. With a comforting voice, she'd tell me that boys were no good and that I would find someone better. After I'd catch my breath, she'd lift my head from her lap for a brief moment, retreat into the kitchen, and return with two double espressos in blue ceramic mugs. She'd wrap my fingers around the warm mug and place her arm around my shoulder. *My sweet girl*, she would say, *everything gets better with a little bit of perspective and a little bit of coffee.*

"Excuse me, miss?" I opened my eyes. The man's voice startled me. "You sure you don't want some coffee?"

I had no time. My director, Monica, would kill me if I were late.

"Yes," I said, surprising myself with the words that came out of my mouth as I walked towards the vendor. "A double espresso, please."

Taking my order, he turned his back again, heating the portafilter handle of the coffee machine before pulling the first shot.

He talked over his shoulder. "Something on your mind, dear?"

"Tonight's the opening night for a musical I'm starring in. A little pre-show jitters. That's all," I said.

He added espresso grounds to the portafilter basket, tapping it a few times for the grounds to settle before sealing them into the machine.

"Well that's a big deal," he said, turning to smile at me. "Looks like I'm talking to the next big star."

I watched as he locked the portafilter in the machine and prepared to extract a double shot of espresso. Whenever I watched Grandma make one, she'd always remind me that 27 seconds was the prime extraction time. Not one second more, not one second less.

The man pressed a button on the machine, keeping his back turned to me as he grabbed a to-go cup from an overhead cupboard. I began counting in my head.

5....6...7....

I felt tears well up in my eyes, elicited by nostalgia. I wished I were back on that porch swing.

10...11...12...

I'd endure another ten heartbreaks if it meant holding a blue ceramic mug around my fingers next to Grandma.

18...19...20...

The man turned around, and I quickly wiped the tears from the corners of my eyes before he could see.

"That'll be two fifty," he said.

I unzipped my purse and handed him my credit card.

29…30…31…

31 seconds.

He shut the machine off, poured the contents, and handed me a small cup of golden-colored froth along with my card.

"There ya go, darling,"

My heart sank but I managed a polite smile. I looked at my watch—I would certainly be late. I took a slight sip. It was way too bitter, not nearly creamy or earthy enough. And not even the slightest hint of a caramel undertone. It was all wrong, and that realization stung.

"Enjoy, sweetheart. And good luck on your show."

"Thanks," I said through a closed smile.

I waited until I was out of his sight before I threw the rest of my coffee in the trash. I hugged my jacket to my body and continued on my way, wondering if I'd have time to buy a dish for the after party, and hoping that Jeff wouldn't forget his line.

Mark Wightman

Waterbaby

We'd got in by squeezing through a hole in the fence. We hang back, under the house, watching the pool guy as he wades through the lake of newly-poured concrete. It sucks at his white rubber boots, like a girlfriend that won't let go. I know what you're thinking. You've got your head tilted in that fuck you way, arms folded across your skinny chest. An untipped French cigarette burns, unsmoked, between your fingers. Blueberry spikes where there used to be a strawberry-blonde ponytail, the skin-art, the metal—you look quite the rebel now.

The guy calls out, trying to flirt. You flash a look at me. Don't say anything. He tries again, scratching at his crotch as he speaks. You lift a middle finger towards him and your expression never changes. He shrugs and laughs. 'Suit yourself.'

For fuck's sake, Ellen, the guy's just trying to be friendly.

Remember that summer, when your mother took us to the pool every day because she was scared shitless to leave you on your own with your pig of an old man again?

Remember the wooden stalls with the half doors like they had in the saloons in those old cowboy movies? How we'd scrunch up on the seats, wooden boards polished smooth by years of backsides, trying to hide so the boys couldn't see us as we changed?

Remember that swimsuit? The hand-me-down from your cousin that was two sizes too big for you? Your mother made a skirt out of some material that she'd cut from one of her old dresses 'to protect your modesty'. You pleaded with her for a new one, but she told you to stop complaining and said you'd grow into it.

Remember that time you let Bobby Madsen put his hand inside it?

Remember how we'd fool around, playing Marco Polo or diving for coins? Then I'd hang from the side of the pool, the pebbledash rough against my skin, as I watched you swim laps. Always backstroke, eyes fixed on the sky. Short, quick strokes at first while you got the feel of it, then longer, reaching back, until eventually it looked like you and the water were one.

Remember how we'd just lie there, floating, letting the sun do its thing? How you'd lift one arm and trace the outline of the clouds with your finger? Where you saw a marshmallow, I saw a shared pillow, but I never said.

Remember what I used to call you?

The guy smooths the concrete till it gleams like burnished metal and puts up a sign that says 'Wet'. You wait till he's back at his truck and then you walk over to the edge of the pool and look down. I know you won't be able to resist. You take off your clothes and fold them neatly at your feet. You climb down the ladder, extending first one tentative foot into the concrete, then the other, getting the feel of it. You lie down, your arms splayed out behind you, a naked sun angel. I watch as you sink slowly into the liquid warmth. You're beautiful. You look up, raise an arm to the sky, and smile.

Pauline Jérémie

Of Gods and Ghosts

When Eva woke up, it was five in the morning, the bed was empty and the sheets cold. It took some time for her eyes to adapt to the darkness, and afterwards she lay in bed staring at the ceiling, her eyelids heavy and her body warming up in the nest of blankets that she had wrapped herself in. She could hear the sound of some show on the television from the living room, along with that of her own measured breathing. With a yawn, she eventually slipped out of bed, searched the floor for her discarded clothes, and put them back on before coming out of the bedroom. The living room was quiet and dark, illuminated only by the occasional burst of light colour from the television screen. Alan was sitting on the sofa, his chest bare and his feet propped up on the coffee table, the bleak light increasing the tired look on his face, making him look older. He turned his head towards Eva when she entered, looked at her for a second, and silently directed his attention back to the television.

Without a word, Eva started making tea. The noise from the television was so low that the clinking of teacups and spoons, the running of water, the sticking of her feet to the lino, everything seemed deafening. She hurried through her task, adding milk to her tea and two sugar cubes to Alan's, spilt some of it onto the counter, and decided to ignore it. She made her way back into the living room, her steps muted on the rough carpet, deposited Alan's cup in front of him on the coffee table, and sat down next to him at the other end of the sofa, hugging her own mug.

The show was a rerun of some sitcom that Alan adored and had already seen every single episode of. Eva took a sip of her tea and, from the corner of her eye, observed Alan's profile. His gaze was fixed on the screen but she could tell that he was not actually paying any attention to the images. He was holding a half-smoked joint in his right hand and seemed to have forgotten about it; the ashes were about to fall onto the sofa, just like they had so many times before. Eva looked down at the tattoo on his bicep, the first one he had ever got—a badly drawn scorpion that had faded into a misshapen lobster—and at the Roman numerals on his chest covered by a thin layer of coarse hair. She had studied those tattoos with the care of a surgeon when they had started dating, along with every other aspect of his body. The lines of the abs that had since long disappeared and made room for the early stages of a beer belly, the bad scar on his left elbow that was the result of a skateboarding accident he had had as a teenager, the hair on his chin and jawline that never seemed to grow past the phase of stubble. Eva still found him as beautiful as she had all those years ago when she had first seen him, but so much had changed now.

"Come here."

The voice was sharp and cut through the silence of the room. Alan had not moved an inch, and for a second Eva thought she had dreamed it. It might have come from the show, she thought, or simply from her imagination. But then Alan tilted his head, an almost imperceptible change in the angle of his neck, beckoning her over.

Eva put her cup down on the coffee table, and slid across the couch until she could feel Alan's body warmth against her arm. What he did next was not unfamiliar, but had become such a rare occurrence that it still surprised Eva, and her body tensed against her will. He simply wrapped his arm around her neck and brought her into a hug, hot and tight and uncomfortable. His forearm pressed against her throat like a vice and her side was bent in a way that hurt her ribs, yet she would not have wanted to be anywhere else in that moment. The mingled smells of weed and Alan's cologne were strong against her nose, and the heat coming from his body made her forget about the cold sheets she had woken up in. She could not remember the last time he had hugged her, or at least the last time he had done so for a reason other than apologising for hurting her, and, as she pressed her body tighter against his, she felt like crying.

Peter Mayne

The Ticket

Your old man's been working the mines as long as you can remember. As a kid you'd watch him come home covered in soot, watch your ma rub his shoulders as he coughed up a storm and complained about the conditions. He did that a lot. Complained. But he never quit. Legend goes that your old man's old man had come when the gold rush was fading and had found the last piece of gold ever dug out of this town, which was used as a down payment for the house. He died in a mining collapse when your old man was fourteen. He started working the mines to provide for his ma and two sisters.

When you're ten a teacher pulls you aside, 'There's been a collapse. Your mother's outside.' You stay at the site day and night. Other wives are there, some buddies from school, too. It takes eight days for your old man and his crew to be rescued. Your ma throws her arms around him, crying. Tells him how stressful it was, that she can't do it again. 'It's me or the mines, John.' 'Minin' is all I know, Mary.' Next morning she's gone. Your old man ran to the station. No trains remained, only their whistles in the distance. At night he lies awake, hearing those whistles whining. There is a picture of her you keep on your desk. She's facing the camera and smiling, but her eyes stare beyond the mountains you know are in the background.

You sit at the kitchen table and watch your old man study his numbers for the coming lottery drawing. He's aged over the years. His hair has thinned. He now wears glasses that barely hang onto the tip of his nose. He folds the ticket into the pocket of his flannel shirt and makes a small sign of the cross. 'Been prayin',' he says. You know later that night he'll say another prayer before sliding the ticket under his pillow. 'What'd you do with all that money?' you ask. 'Invest it.' 'The hell you know 'bout investin', Pa?' you say.

You're the first in the family to graduate high school. Your old man wears his only suit. You hope that your ma will show up. Give a reason why she left. Tell you what she's been doing, that she's missed you. But she doesn't. Afterwards, you and your old man walk home. Neither of you talk. He knows you plan on taking time off to work. You start working construction the next week.

The work is hard. Every morning at dawn you have a coffee with your old man. Neither of you say much. 'Thinkin' 'bout moving to be closer to work,' you say one morning. He sips his coffee, nods. 'Need anythin' you let me know,' he says while placing his hand on your shoulder. You get along with your coworkers. Some you know from school. Older ones tell you to go to college. 'You don' wanna be doin' this at my age,' they say.

The new place is small. It's above a bar. Sleep is hard to come by. You and Nicole tell yourselves it's only temporary. 'We'll move soon,' you say. You take Nicole to a restaurant high in the mountains your coworkers told you about. 'Your lady deserves it,' they said. After dinner you walk her to the porch outside that overlooks the mountainside. Far below you can see the town lit up. Neither of you have ever been this far from home before. She takes your hand, 'I'm pregnant.' When you tell your old man he just nods and looks out the window, beyond the mountains in the background. He knows you'll never get out. Neither will Nicole.

One day you're out paving a road. The boss pulls you aside, 'There's been an accident.' A few hours later your old man's body is found. The funeral procession is small, mainly coworkers. 'Hardest worker there ever was,' they tell you. Their wives have the same look of fear your ma had years ago. The house you'll never own was left to you. You and Nicole move back in to be closer to the school—your son starts soon. You were also left his meager savings. A man who had nearly worked his entire life left with almost nothing to show for it.

Your old man had never followed his dreams. You don't even know what they were. 'He jus' provided, was all he knew,' you tell Nicole. You realize how little you do know of that man. You wish you had asked more questions, wish you had spent more time with him. You don't know when you began to pity him—the man who worked and knew nothing else—and distance yourself. You don't even know what you pitied. Maybe it was the lifelessness in his eyes, or the tiredness in his movements. Maybe it was the way his back slumped when he sat, or the way he stared beyond the mountains in the background, his glasses barely hanging on. You visit his grave on the way back from work and let your old man know the real you, always beginning with, 'Hello, Pa.'

You walk your son to school on his first day—the same one you went to. Some friends and coworkers are there. You wave, so do they. You take Adam to his class. 'Learn somethin',' you say. 'Find your dream.' Putting your hand on his shoulders you say: 'One day you'll understan'.' You then go buy a lottery ticket. That night you'll say a prayer before putting it under your pillow. You've realized that the lottery ticket was never for your old man. It was for you. It was his small hold on hope. Hope that maybe you can get out of this town. That year half the construction crew is laid off. 'Ain' nobody buildin' down 'ere,' you're told. You begin working the mines.

Temi Oh

Do You Dream of Terra-Two?

[excerpt from a longer work]

By the time they drove out to the shuttle, they had been in their space-suits so long that they were all beginning to sweat. Mission control, the band, the cheering crowd, the screen which read T-minus-ninety minutes—it all disappeared from the rear window as the made their way to the open stretch of land where the rockets were chained to the earth. As they approached, Astrid realised that they were far bigger than she remembered. The size of a cathedral. The little crew module was attached to huge, propellant-filled towers which would provide the thrust to hurl them through the atmosphere. When Astrid climbed out of the van she was at the foot of the giant; it hissed and thrummed, and steam curled off its steel surface like breath through parted lips.

They took the elevator up sixty meters to the orbiter access arm and Astrid felt the drop in her stomach as they left the ground behind. She knew that thirty seconds of acceleration was nothing compared to the flight which awaited her on the other side of the shuttle's hatch, where they would soar to twenty-six times the speed of sound in eight minutes.

The elevator door slid open to a sunlit bridge where they were greeted by the close-out crew, who led them along the walkway and into the shuttle. The hatch was a little circular door and climbing in was an inelegant process which required Astrid to get on all fours and then to roll onto her back, every movement a struggle in her heavy suit; she felt like a diver wearing a second skeleton. It occurred to her, as the crew fumbled to strap her in, that these were the last people she would see on Earth, and she didn't even know their names.

Once they finished, Astrid was tied down so tightly she could feel the pulse throbbing in her legs. Her ears were filled with the chatter of mission control. "As you know: I've done this a few times," Commander Sheppard said with a smile. "It's over quickly. Your job is just to take it all in."

Something strange and wonderful occurred to Astrid then. The fight was over. For the first time in her life, even if she did nothing at all, she would be in space.

It was her testimony, almost, the day she discovered Terra-Two. Astrid had grown up knowing that there was a distant planet outside her own solar system, a green twin of Earth orbiting dual stars. But the first day that a longing to go there awoke inside her, she had been in assembly. All the children in her year group and the one above had been ushered into the main hall to watch a video. It was part of a presentation given by a team from the UKSA. "Another habitable planet," one of them announced to the darkened room, and the screen lit up with dazzling vistas of an alien land. Astrid saw an ocean, lush mountain ranges, and terracotta canyons ridged like clay fire shells.

"They call it a 'New Earth'," said the young geologist with exaggerated air-quotes, "but our findings actually suggest that Terra-Two is many billions of years older than our own Earth. Truly, *we're* living on Terra-Two."

Under the collar of her shirt, Astrid's neck prickled with goosebumps. She sat up rigidly, as if she had been called by name, and in a way she had. This, they told her, was a place for the intrepid. The first settlers would not arrive until they were middle-aged. Their job would be to chart terrain, and to explore the land, to name the secret schools of fish which swept through the coral reefs, and photograph night-blooming flowers. Someone in this room, they said in a reverent whisper, may be the first to set foot in the crystalline caves which had formed underground. Astrid imagined herself descending and seeing her own aged face reflected in the frosty mineral beams.

This was a job for the brave, they said, a job for dreamers, for people who, like Astrid, woke every morning longing for another world. "Imagine it," the recruiter said. She had.

That week she bounced around with the hyper energy of a new convert. She would get into Dalton, she told herself; she would be accepted into the Beta and she would go to Terra-Two.

Astrid would remember the years after that assembly and before the launch as a single shining line of triumph. The shortest route between point A, the naming of her desire, and point B, leaving Earth—its sole zenith of realisation.

Later, they would ask what she had been thinking when the hatch slammed shut. Had she been contemplating what a slow labour their mission was, how many minds and hands it had taken to get her to this point, to this two minute launch window? Or was she counting every sacrifice, every year of her life she had given and was still to give?

As the flight director commenced the countdown she heard Professor Stenton's measured voice crackle through the headset. "Take care of yourself," she said, which she said whenever she bid them goodbye before a school trip or the start of a holiday, standing in the driveway with the sun in her eyes.

They would ask Astrid if she had been afraid and she would answer "no" every time. And if she ever looked back at the strange arc of her life and wondered if any moment had ever been as perfect as dreaming of it, she would say, "that one."

The shuttle launched. Astrid burst through the luminescent atmosphere and into the black firmament beyond. She had been longing to leave her whole life, and finally nothing was standing between her and the stars. Not a selection committee, not a mean twist of fate, twenty-three years battling the loneliness of space, or the hopelessness.

Teresa Lee

Missing

[excerpt from a longer work]

The summer lingered into late September that year. Employees were lured out onto the office complex's trimmed grass during their lunch hours to warm their air-conditioned skin with natural UV rays. A world away, in the skyscraper-dense City—two-hour's drive distant—the same heat would oppress. But here was a small corporate oasis, hemmed in by green fields dotted with sheep and cut through with A roads, where the sunshine made of the surroundings a veritable picture postcard.

It had been one such sunny day when Millie went missing. She had gone for a walk around the perimeter a little after 2pm. That was when her teammates remembered her leaving her desk and when Aadesh saw her walk into the undergrowth. He quietly maintained that that was what he saw, in spite of his colleagues' scepticism. Later, when the pile of neatly folded clothes belonging to Millie was found in the bushes, everyone was obliged to believe him. Aadesh often felt that his colleagues looked askance at him after that; or perhaps he was just being paranoid. Projecting his usual outsider feelings onto their muted, but justifiably disturbed and perfectly normal, British reactions.

The offices of The Company were a new complex of four large beige buildings, whose every feature, from the colour of the walls to the shape of the desks, was consciously engineered to optimise workers' motivation, productivity, problem-solving skills and sense of belonging. Stretches of manicured grass lined the walkways connecting the buildings, and a pond, fondly referred to as "the lake" sat in the centre, with a resident family of ducks. A leafy, tree-lined walkway ran around the complex's perimeter.

In the air hung a sense of serene modernity, and important business being done behind closed doors. Men in suits and women in stylish dresses moved around the premises, going from meeting to desk to coffee break to desk again, laptops and smartphones in tow. Harassed, overworked sighs interspersed polite conversation as colleagues strolled along or rattled off milestones and quarterly reviews into their handsets. A peal of laughter would ring out above the other sounds for a moment; a masculine "ha-ha-ha!" A cough. A comment about the unseasonal good weather.

—

"Where's Millie?"

Philip stood frowning over the empty chair. She had not shown up for their performance review meeting. It was 5.30pm. Her laptop screensaver had long faded to black and beside it sat a half-finished paper cup of coffee, her mobile phone, and a pair of earphones. Her handbag was on the floor beside her chair.

Kirsty, never far away, bustled over, holding her laptop aloft with one arm while tugging down her too-tight pencil skirt with the other.

"I don't know!" she said. "I pinged her three times. I need a spreadsheet from her."

Reece, who was sitting at the far end of the desk in an online conference call, shrugged and shook his head.

"Aadesh?" Philip asked the quiet young Indian, who was sitting nearby, apparently absorbed in his screen. Aadesh looked up.

"I haven't seen her for some hours," he replied.

Philip looked around the wide open-plan office space, nonplussed, absently running a hand through his greying hair. He noticed Kirsty watching and dropped his hand.

"Very strange," he muttered, turning away. Kirsty moved to his side.

"What's going on?"

Liz appeared, ambling in that slow, rolling walk of hers. She was so large that she rocked from side to side as she advanced, the skirt of her oversized floral dress swishing back and forth. She held a box of Jaffa cakes in her hand and Philip found himself staring at them, then immediately felt guilty. It was unprofessional to judge—her eating habits were none of his business, and she was an efficient worker, which was all that should matter.

"Millie's gone AWOL," Kirsty said. "We can't call her. Her phone is here."

Philip realised he was gritting his teeth, and quickly released his jaw. He told himself that Kirsty didn't choose to have an American accent. Or that voice. He wasn't usually so easily annoyed by her; he was just stressed. His boss had been on his back all week for a deadline. That must be it.

"Oh dear," Liz said, taking a Jaffa cake from the box and inserting it into her small mouth. She took a bite, then said through the mouthful, "When was the last time anyone saw her?"

"I saw her here when I got back from lunch," Kirsty said.

"I've been in meetings all day," Philip shrugged.

Aadesh said nothing.

Aadesh hesitated a second too long, and then Kirsty spoke again, and the moment vanished. It felt silly to say, "I saw her walk into some bushes." He felt distant enough from his colleagues as it was.

He liked Millie. She had made the effort to learn to pronounce his name properly, when so many people butchered it with bizarre, lazy variations. This would have scandalised his parents back in India who had chosen it for their precious only son, who was 23 and living alone and abroad for the first time.

When Aadesh was growing up in Mumbai, England had always seemed faraway but familiar; the colonial legacy hung over his life like distant clouds. The reality of living here was something else. The English was spoken either in an accent that he had only heard on language learning tapes at school, or else in an unfamiliar, coarse accent he had trouble comprehending. The weather was drab and the food bland and overpriced. This small town was calm and clean, but compared to his frenetic hometown, felt also lifeless and bleak. He often had to remind himself to say "thank you" and "sorry" more often.

"Want one?" Liz proffered the box of Jaffa cakes to Aadesh, who shook his head with a small smile of thanks. He noticed Philip staring at the box in Liz's hand; he obviously wanted one but was too polite to ask.

Zoë Ramsey

The Letter M

'My sister's not feeling well, so I'm going to make her some medicine,' Madison announced as she plodded off toward the low cabinet housing the plastic cups. 'Is that okay, Mommy and Daddy? I want to help put stuff away, but I feel really bad about sissy!'

'Of course, Maddie!' Sophie said. 'Daddy and I can put away the groceries. Your sister will be better soon, but your medicine will certainly help. What are you going to put in it?' Sophie and Ken began unpacking the plastic bags the mother and daughter had just brought in.

'Hmm. I don't know. When I'm sick, you give me that sticky purple stuff. I don't like that so much. I'm going to make something else. Something yummy.' Madison tapped her chin in thought. 'I know, I'll start with honey!'

'Great idea! Then what will you add?' Sophie smiled as she put a bag of peaches in the fruit bowl next to the microwave.

'Mommy, I need time to think!' Madison furrowed her brow for a moment. 'How about milk?'

'Oh, she'll like that.' Sophie took the milk from the refrigerator and set it on the table next to Madison while Ken continued to flit around the kitchen with boxes and bags.

'Thanks Mommy. I can't wait to give it to her.' Madison stuck her tongue out while she concentrated on pouring the milk carefully into the cup until it was half full. Then she began to stir it, three strokes clockwise, three counterclockwise. 'Mommy?'

'Yes, sweetie?'

'Do you think she'll stop being sad soon?'

'Of course! Do you remember the last time you were sad?'

'Erm, I think so.' Maddie put the spoon down and went to the cupboard. After a moment, she returned to the table with a box of cocoa powder. She dumped a large spoonful into the cup and stirred. Three strokes clockwise, three counterclockwise. 'I think it was when Robert at school broke my favourite pencil. But it was an accident, so I wasn't mad. Just a little sad that I don't have my favourite pencil anymore.'

'And are you still sad?'

'I guess not.'

'See? People are only sad for a little while before they forget about it or something good happens again.'

'You're right.' Maddie returned the cocoa powder and came back to the table with a jar of peanut butter. She added one spoonful to the cup. Then she stirred. Three strokes clockwise, three counterclockwise. 'Can I put a peach in the medicine, Mommy?'

Sophie looked at the cup and the lumpy, brown mixture within, then at Madison's eager face. 'I don't know about that, sweetheart. I don't think a peach would taste very nice with all of that. How about we wait and have them all together as a family tomorrow?'

Madison pursed her lips. 'But Mommy, I really want to give her a peach. It's healthy!'

'Madison,' Ken warned.

Madison's face relaxed. 'Okay,' she said quickly. 'All together as a family is a better idea. You're right. Hey, Mommy?'

'Yes, sweetheart?'

'Can we take my sister out to the movies when she stops being sad? Then she can be happy again,' Madison asked. Ken and Sophie exchanged a look. Ken opened his mouth to speak, but Sophie cut him off.

'I think that's a wonderful idea, baby. I bet she'd love to go.'

'Hey now, don't I get a say in this?' Ken chimed in, a bit too cheerfully.

'Daddy, you always say yes! That's why I asked Mommy instead.'

Ken laughed. 'You're right, rugrat. I can't say no to my little princess.'

'Mind it'll be a while, Maddie. Your sister is still very unwell. I'm not sure how soon we can go.'

'That's okay, mommy. I don't mind waiting.'

'Now finish up that medicine and we'll bring it through to her,' Ken encouraged.

'Okay, Daddy!' Maddie jumped down from the table and took the cup in her hand. She walked slowly towards the hall, taking care not to spill anything while Sophie and Ken followed her. 'Will you open the door for me, Mommy?'

'Sure, sweetheart.' The door swung inward. Muffled crying came from the bed in the corner of the room.

'Sissy, I bringed you some medicine!'

'Brought,' Sophie corrected gently.

'Sissy, I brought you some medicine!' The crying continued as the small family approached the bed. 'I'll just leave it on your table so you can have it whenever you want!' Maddie placed it carefully onto the night stand, between the lamp and the framed family photo where Ken, Sophie and Madison beamed at the camera, but the youngest child kept her gaze lowered.

'Say thank you to your sister,' Sophie said.

'Thank you for the medicine, Madison.' The small voice broke as she spoke. The young girl sat up for the first time and looked at the three people in front her. Her white eyes shone brightly against her brown skin and her black hair stuck out at every angle. 'Please let me go home now. Please. I'm a good girl, I said thank you. Please!' Tears ran down her face as she begged.

'Please what?'

'Please…M-M-Mommy.'

Ken let out a small laugh. 'You cost a pretty penny, chocolate chip. You're staying right here.'

'Sweetheart, you are home,' Sophie added. 'This is your home now. Now drink your medicine up, it'll help you feel better. And when you stop crying, your sister would love to take you out to the cinema! Wouldn't that be nice?'

The girl choked back a sob. 'Yes…Mommy.'

'There's a good girl,' Sophie looked down at the small child lovingly.

'Alright, Maddie.' Ken interjected. 'We'll let your sister rest and us three can think up a new name for her! Jane is just so…boring, don't you think?'

'Oh yes, can we?' Maddie jumped with excitement. 'I think it should be something like mine! How about something that starts with the letter M also?' They retreated from the room as Maddie listed names.

'Molly, Mary, Monica, Marcy…'

poetry

Alyson Kissner

Underearth

Make me a fossil. Make me ancient
And indispensible. Don't touch me

With your hands. Make tools for me
And classifications, and bodies and
                                        bodies of seas.

Unburden me. Tell me I'm rare.
Tell me I'm dead, and you've made me
Living
        again.

I am proof there was something before us.
I am traces of animals and species and plants,
Petrified,
        but stout-hearted.

Obtain me by digging.
I am beyond time but I can be dated.
How did I evolve? Decay? You can tell me

My age, my number—the number of lives
I've held
                                in my teeth.

We all have signals, soft tissues.
As bone, I hollow this value.

I have been deposited in rivers
And found you, dreaming in mud.

Azra Tabassum

Sugar Plum

I love that you are fingers first,
plum-soaked and
sodden with it.

Your want
and mine,
a choke-chain around that delirious hum

That pull and heave,
whisky-dipped tied twice
around your fist

Tied once over
and over and over, full of the throat,
the untwined spine, the mouth

On mouth and teeth
and tongue, unloosen the back,
undo the shoulders and press down

Hand-first, landlocked
fish the breath out of the stomach,
swallow it whole, take it

Bellyful, mouth full,
unlearn the ache, cup the bruise
kiss downwards against those plains

Sigh – honestly,
breathless, and begin the careful
unravelling, unstitch the skin again

And again, I love
how you tighten your fingers
around it, bring it closer and

let it fill you, brimming.

Jacqueline Thompson

Matryoshka

I was red hot once, in my sarafan, with my six
pretty girls beside me. We had nothing to hide,
our lacquered simpers graced the mantelpiece,
our bellies round with pride. Then hands split
us apart, our wooden waists howling, crammed
my bean of a babe into her big sister, and she
into hers, and she into hers, and she into hers.

They made an onion of us, and we had to
eat each other's secrets. We'd grown old,
the vintage of our curls and beauty spots,
flushed cheeks and bitten lips, had bred
contempt. We little ladies had taken up
too much space, for much too long.

My body solid with devoured kin,
they placed me in a modest place to
squat beneath a lampshade, vie for
prominence with porcelain tat, the
vacant milk-skinned shepherdess.

Now I cannot move for the heft
of my girls. I retch when they
wriggle within me. My glaze
has cracked, my paint flakes.

My lashes fall. My cheeks
blanche. The flowers of
my sarafan are wilting.

My rosy smile has
shrunk to a bitter

black dot.

Krystal Foster

(After the Reading) To Rita Dove:

When you spoke, it wasn't
an automation.

The words were backed

by multiplicities
and thick

with subterranean love.

We were never lonely
in them, or misdirected.

That was the shock of it.

We had been taught
to deflect:

to handle our affection
like politicians, speaking

too well and almost
too carefully

in the crisp rooms.

Lauren Pope

Mescaline For Breakfast

Time strips in sheaths
of falling clothes –
I think I know that man,
and then he disappears
into the wall
and I am alone
lying at the bottom
of an inflatable raft,
skin plasticized by lamplight,
fixated on the things
I have carried with me all these years –
the cups of my palms
are two blue pools
and the deeper I look, the more
questions they throw up.

Marianne MacRae

The Book Of

In the beginning, we went to a pearl
and asked for forgiveness.
The pearl glittered and said,
"Let he who is without a stone cast the first line."
And with that, fishing was born
and all the people were saved.

The rooster sang a song of the morning,
his pockets full of feathers.
Men rose from their beds
cocking their guns in time with the melody.
And the people rejoiced
for the rooster was silenced.

And there was evening.
We cut stars from our skin
and cooked them to a stew
so the people might taste
the darkness of the universe.
When we served the meal,
they sat back and thought it was good.

competition
winners

Dominic Hale

ON THE FLYLEAF OF MACDIARMID'S *COLLECTED POEMS*

eftir C.M. Grieve

Sloan Prize Winner 2016

I

A'm no' cut oot fae this:
a faimished warldlin'
an' a reiver; chorin', laithful Sassenach;
imperial gellie weirin'
a guise; scranner o' yir Lallans leed,
this screed
ill-tonguit. Repeat, say ower this:
I' the how-dumb-deid
Pish! Ach,
a couldna read.

A'm mair mim-moued 'an ye,
auld birsie, atterin' Hugh (or no'), ay ye,
O drouthy, hairy, rampin' baird,
an' a'm juist as fause! Skeichin', a sing
appropriation, a sling
a deifie at the braes o' rimie
hillheids, tenements, the
postcaird lochs, the blaey
burns an' whins o' tourist boards.

O' coorse AUSTERITY's
a schame, a scam, a pit-on, an' a lee,
a wheen o' blethers
ay, a chitterin' ideology!

An' baws to dreichit POETRY,
an' baws to langed-for UNITY,
an' baws to branded YESirees:

ay, Thistle dae it nice-er-ly
(an' ayeways tak the wather
wi' ye).

An' a think that mebbe at last we
ken wir aw in this thegither,
sae come alang, ma pals: lat's aw gang kick a Tory!

II

o' the cauld hairst nicht
cochlin cochlin clocher commaund thir elements
The warl' like an eemis stane
hack hack
Wags i'
hack
the lift;
Hast thoo, ~~spirit~~ ghaistie,
Perform'd tae pynt the ~~tempest~~ on-ding tha' a bad thee
An' my eerie memories fa'
Like a yowdendrift
we canna save oor voices frae the wund. Skirlin'
the skailwind yirdit;
the hale watter yirdit;
wirds driftin' oan wirds;
the 'real unabstract' snaw;

i' the rairie cloods' skellochin'
ye swatch the pus o' wickit Joseph Stalin,
aw the aby
deid o' riven centuries;
snaw an' blash, brickle, fawin'.

Synthetic airt!
Like a yowdendrift so's ~~I~~ a couldna read
an' a couldna read an' a couldna read
The ~~words~~ wirds *cut oot i' the stane*
cut oot
Had the fug o' fame
fuck up cut oot

An' ~~history~~'s hazelraw
the smittin' stain
No' yirdit thaim.
Cut oot.

III

Deid, perfervid bastart, leave!
Yir sleekit langage is a stourie tuim! Tha's
me. Fareweel awmichtie seil, God bliss.
A willna greet, or grieve.

The Sloan Prize is awarded annually for a prose or verse composition in Lowland Scots vernacular to a matriculated student or to a graduate of the University of Edinburgh of less than three years' standing.

Marianne MacRae

January Diary

Grierson Verse Prize Winner 2016

1st
Midday, the flat quiet, city still
giving up the ghost of a headache.
Ate eggs with bread and two painkillers.

4th
Morning spent Googling types of snake,
listless trips to the kettle for more tea -
the dog flotsam in a dressing-gown's wake.

Thumb locked in the jaw of a guidebook on grief.

6th
On the Meadows with a Spanish stranger
discussing his Bichon Frise. He showed me

one of its paws up close, rearranging
fur and dirt to reveal three toes missing.
"The street foxes here are dangerous,

but really, he is stupid. He offers a kiss
to the devil, I think?" The dog's black eyes
were two LPs playing on the distance.

8th
Last night the kitchen caught fire
and in the smoke I thought I saw you.

11th
Bowie dead at 69.

Mum called, asked if I remembered playing you
a cassette tape of *Heroes* every day
in the hospital? I said I try not to.

14th
In the news a kangaroo held the grey
sagging head of his lover. I want to believe
it was grief and not a mating display,

because even if he killed her, can't he
want her back?

18th
In this month of bare trees I always feel

like I'm forgetting a birthday. Track
the calendar with a finger, get lost
in boxes too small and can't relax.

20th
Blackford Hill this morning, sky unwashed,
it hovered over the hoar-frosted
grass where the dog ran to exhaustion.

Now he wakes only to be fed or
briefly patted, before shambling
back to the bathroom, dropping

at the altar of the sink, limbs angled
in something like worship.

23rd
A drive out of the city's evening tangle,

car speeding across the ink-stained slip
of tree shrugged B-roads. There are three hundred
and forty two days of this year left to live.

26th
The maternal reaction to her dead
offspring was not as prolonged as that shown
by [insert own mother's name instead] –

a giraffe baby died four years ago,
the memory of it resounding
in my browser window.

27th
Plunger on the cafetière sounds
like the Titanic sinking. Coffee pours
and two wanton spoons of sugar drown.

29th
Ate too many Twiglets, trying to gorge
myself back to a life in the woods.
Do twigs remember being trees or

are they just dead? Not sure I would
want to spend the afterlife so close
to the body that betrayed me, would you?

31st
Took two painkillers with eggs on toast,
the scramble laid out like a white brain
on a white bed in need of diagnosis.

The Grierson Prize is awarded to a matriculated student of the University of Aberdeen or the University of Edinburgh for a composition in any recognized verse form but not 'free verse'.

Quentin Scobie

Erica

Lewis Edwards Prize Winner 2016

Erica thinks something in Italian.

The Italian becomes weird Italian.

Erica says to herself "o.k. urgh o.k. come on. o.k. let's go." Sliding out of the duvet, stepping onto the coarse blue carpet of her room, keeping her arms folded like wings to her breasts, she finds her tights, underwear and bra, and returns immediately to the warmth of her bed. The pyjamas are slowly exchanged for these slightly colder clothes, and she begins to feel more awake. The slightly colder clothes warm up. Temperature is essential to movement, as in the morning, humans are practically cold-blooded. Erica dislikes all things cold-blooded. She dislikes being "in the morning".

Erica gets out of bed again. She looks at the blood stains on her mattress and thinks something in Italian, somewhere between a thought of cosmic tragedy in having a body, and a numb checklist-ready reminder of how long she has been sleeping in these sheets.

She chooses clothes with the analytic tension that occasions from having to pick clothes for yourself. The trousers are black, and hug her legs tightly, with the tights worn underneath, to make a doubly tight hugging. In the interests of warmth many women do this, slinky armouring motions of hands moving up legs, early in the mornings of cold countries. This is a normal, yet clandestine, activity. Erica finds herself in a cold country doing this regularly.

She assesses her look in the full-length mirror where, with forever an oscillation of attraction and repulsion, there is a propensity for increased repulsion in the morning when one feels like shit. Erica does this, feeling both unattractive and attractive, focussing on her face and imprinting its matrix of eyes, nose and mouth so that she may have a good idea of what other people are looking at as she interacts with them during the day. She then goes to the bathroom mirror and does the same thing, here the light different, harshly scrutinising her scalp from above. Erica has an interesting hairline, in that it is indecisive. The majority of the hair goes back, but some shorter strands stay in little sways. She takes the plastic covering off her toothbrush, and then puts on the toothpaste, then she wets the toothpaste under the tap, then she starts to brush her teeth.

Her mind wanders, always in Italian, wanders wanders wanders. As she looks at herself she imagines how she would look in ten years, twenty, thirty, merely and vaguely older. This imagination exercise functions not in sections, but as a deliberate calibration of her mother's face over her own. She sees her tiredness shaping her future, until her eventual death of course, but she is not horrified. It does not occur to her to be horrified, almost lacking another eye to be horrified for. She spits out the toothpaste, watching it oyster its way under the dome of the plughole protector.

Erica urinates. In a sense she is urinating in Italian. There is not much to describe here, as she is a woman she does not have the privilege of watching the stream of urine, as it penetrates the pool of toilet water. She does not have the privilege of skirting the edge of the pool with the stream and creating plopping sound effects that alternate with intensity dependent on the distance from the pool's edge. Women tend to just sit and focus on some object in their vision, at least, that's what I imagine they would do. Perhaps some close their eyes in the confidence of not missing the bowl—something men cannot do. Bodily fluids are difficult to narrate artistically, and perhaps this should change, but I am not going to spend all my time narrating Erica's toilet trips. You, reader, must use your imagination for the most part, and could extend your speculation to the toilet trips of all people you know. What are they thinking about? Whatever Erica was thinking, it was most probably in Italian.

Erica puts on perfume. Erica puts rash cream on little skin irritations that have appeared on her neck and shoulder area. As she inspects she gives them guilty scratches. Eventually the fingers move, downwards, towards other things — a door handle — along a white corridor wall — another door handle — one of those Italian percolators with the funny cartoon man pointing upwards, the handle of that — the fridge door handle — the coffee bag saying "LAVAZZA" — the percolator again, unscrewing it and making it clean for another round of coffee bean dirt — the tap, which is slightly broken, only that it doesn't seem to have any stability or attachment to the sink — the twisty heat changer knob on the cooker. She waits for the coffee by finding the biscotti. The biscotti is the biscuits in Italian. Italian people seem to love biscuits, and thus biscotti. "Biscotti", as a word and an idea, is big in Italy. Erica eats a biscuit.

The percolator with the funny cartoon, squat, silver, hot, hotter. It has the delightful shape of two trapeziums touching heads. Underneath it the dark grey circular plate of the electric cooker. When this thing gets hot it's completely incognito you know, dangerous invisible hotness. People brush their hands on these grey circles and say "Ah! Hot!" and they get a little mad at the inert object, as though it had meant to trick them.

Erica drinks coffee. Erica cools the coffee with her breath, pressurised by the tiniest "o" opening in her "bocca". "Bocca" means mouth in Italian. The pool of the coffee blown from the edge generates a ballet of eddies, circulating into the centre. Spirals of aroma navigate their way to Erica's nasal cave. The nose in Italian is "naso". Erica's nose is petit, symmetrical and very touchable. One is regularly inclined to poke Erica's nose on the tip and wiggle it slightly, its internal structure seems designed to accommodate this. A delicious conk.

To what extent are we attracted to these gimmicks huh? Moving about the "matrix" of features like my narrative is built upon anatomy? Now I should probably talk about her "occhios", the brown eyes of canine softness. Yes, she has brown eyes. My mum asked me once what colour were Erica's eyes. I couldn't remember, but I supposed they were brown. The dark warmth of the brown eyes was what I remembered, not the colour. My mum said that most Italians had brown eyes. We concluded they must be brown, and when I checked, we were right. The "occhios" go to the fridge and pick up the lactose free milk, milk called "Lacto-free", and pour it into the black liquid iris until it is the colour of themselves. Erica drinks coffee.

When Erica walks, the corridor becomes hers — its long sloped whiteness forming a tunnel for her thought. She is on her phone, using it to facilitate the line of movement, like a sleek black skateboard for her mind. Noticing what is otherwise un-noticed creates a bumpy ride, it could accumulate to a noise that can be terrify in the wrong places. The iPhone is a smooth seat for the soul. On WhatsApp her friends are made out of emoji, one a pizza slice, another two fish-shaped flags of blue and red. I think the emoji she uses for me is an unimpressed face with closed eyes, a yellow circle with three horizontal lines. What a crazy world we live in! Somewhere, not far away, a mountain is covered in snow. Shrubhill, the newly-built student accommodation where Erica did all this waking and brushing and drinking and thinking in Italian, is silent — an empty white pressure.

Erica turns left at the end of the corridor, left again past the red "Dry Riser Inlet", past a badly fitted electrical socket turned 90°, and through the door to the staircase. On the ceiling, a weirdly shaped plastic protrusion senses her movement, and switches on the lights.

The staircase is newfangled and seems to jut out of the fuzzy blue carpet. It is formed from beige non-offensive wood and black metal tubes and bars. Erica's face glows each time she passes an ovoid light, bulging like white tumours from the walls, greeting her one by one as she descends. Actually I'm not sure "white tumours" is the right way to describe these ovoid lights, as they are not as sinister as tumours, but not as benign as eggs. Erica passes and passes, still on her iPhone probably, or maybe just beginning to think about the walking or what awaits her at university.

She goes round some more corners, with the painted white bricks and more beige wood, now doors. She goes past an ugly red "futuristic" looking sofa, which looks as though it were designed by someone who studied product design, that is, badly designed (haha! :D) . She presses a swollen green button for the main door and enters into the cold morning air. Oh! The Cold Morning Air! The way it operates on the senses; the wind as your extra ethereal ice-vest, rummaging through the sinuses and down the "collo" and "culo". It is the wind that delivers the temperature to us. In Italy there is a breeze, but in Edinburgh, there is the wind.

I think Erica takes the bus most of the time. I think she thinks in Italian, "I'm going to take the bus". She waits for a few minutes with the rest of the "Morning Bus People" who I regularly see waiting for the bus when I go to class in the morning. What do you think they're all thinking? It's all Italian to me, unspoken foreign languages in closed circuits, a different kind of bodily fluid, somehow rippling back. Now Erica is on the bus, the first moment of true human physical contact with the bus driver, saying "Thank you" as she places the exact change in the strange clunky slot and takes the ticket that prints out like a tongue. I don't really know what Erica listens to in the morning, but I'm going to pretend its this funky obscure Japanese music I listen to, to feel self-important and different from everyone. So we can imagine Erica listening to this slightly kooky Japanese funk from the 80s, with the grey city gyrating around her from the top deck of the bus. People going in and out of doors, harassed by each other, the Tesco express harassed by the newly opened Sainsbury's down the road, yeah yeah yeah, empty urban harassment, it's all harassment 'til ∞...

Someone else pings the pingy thing that makes the bus stop. Erica descends the bus stairs, veering a little as the gravity adjusts with the bus' reduction in speed. She leaves the bus doors, says thank you to the bus driver. Yes, when you do this sort of stuff alone in real life it is as though you are the blandest, most robotic entity you can ever be. There is a desperation of neutrality in moving past the bus driver, conducting yourself appropriately with the logistical operations of transport. Human bodies harassed by their own empty mechanisms. We say "thank you" as a sort of "thank God" — thank God you are letting me out again, out of this tight hard metal thing that pushes itself along and around its route. Erica doesn't think this, but feels it.

Edinburgh feels like a larger tight hard metal thing, sometimes. It is all around her. The street is high definition in the morning light, the sky is now a rare blue. AzzzzzzzzzUUUUUUrroooo, sings the sky. The people of the street never look as though they are hearing the pleasant blueness sung. The city: unknown dogs, unknown children, muscles bubbling to tiring shapes; muscles of flesh, muscles of stone, faces forming other faces. Human "fagioli", forever. Bean soup, and soup, and the sound of soup, and the sperm race, and the endless continuation of the sperm race. She walks — past the bagpipe tack, the "alternative culture" tack and the Costa Coffee "people drinking coffee in the windows" tack. There is a lot of bullshit (as noun, verb and adjective) going on in the city. And pigeon shit. The pigeons limp unperturbed on their stumps.

Erica doesn't really like pigeons because she thinks they are full of diseases. She sits alone in her 9 am lecture on Chinese Literature, thinking about why she's here, worrying about her thoughts, biting the frosting of dead skin around her nails. She must watch the film "Red Sorghum" as her homework. She thinks about how different it is to have a lecture here in Edinburgh, rather than in Bologna, where people are warmer. Around her, the ocean of proud twenty-somethings, preening, pretending to look like they are not looking at each other. Shrubhill Student Accommodation is about 25 minutes away, and the weather is changing.

Later she says to me: "Yes, in our world we will just smoke weed and have sex, then wake up at 4 and go to sainsbury's, eat biscotti. You know like Anarchism."

She does a little revolutionary arm jerk for effect.

I say "So what we do now… so basically Shrubhill."

She laughs and says "Yes, a world of Shrubhills."

I say "A world of Shrubhills."

Internally something is set into spasm by this thought of comfort and love, and tiny rooms of coarse blue carpet, bubbles spanning the world in white corridors. The radiator was on four, I was lying in a pool of sweat on her bed.

A world of Shrubhills.

This prize was established in memory of Lewis Edwards, who died while a student of English Literature at the University. It is open to any matriculated undergraduate student of the University of Edinburgh.

Zoë Ramsey

Fights an Hings

Sloan Prize Winner 2016

'Robert! Your pal's at the door!'

That's my Ma. She's always shoutin at me. Only she calls me Robert. All ma pals call me Rab. I go doon the stair to see who it is. Ma stops me first.

'Have you done your homework?'

'Aye, I done it.'

'Gies it. I want tae see it.'

'Och, Ma. It cannae wait?'

'Go an get it. Or you're no goin' oot.'

'Can ah no see who's at the door first, no?'

'Dinnae be cheeky. Hurry up.'

It's wee Fraser at the door. 'Alright, mate?'

'Alright, pal?' he says. Wee Fraser's a year under me at school. He's Jill's bairn, who's pals wi Ma. I like wee Fraser. He's a bit thick sometimes, but hard as.

'Two seconds, mate.' I leave wee Fraser at the door an run up the stair. I take ma homework to my Ma who's watchin' Countdown. She never turned the radio aff, I dinnae ken how she can watch telly wi the radio on. That new song aboot walkin like Egyptians is playin. 'You need tae sign it, Ma.'

'You dinnae ken how tae say please, Robert?'

'Ma, please go an sign ma homework.'

'Alright, Robert.' She takes a pen fae the wee table next tae her chair an signs it. 'Mind your faither's hame at six. He'll no want you oot when he gets hame.'

'Aye Ma, ah ken. I'm no daft, like. You told me this mornin.'

'Dinnae, Robert.' She looks shattered. Her chequebook's sittin on the wee table where she got the pen. Probably why she looks like shite. We're skint, as usual. 'Go an play with your pals.'

I go to the door an wee Fraser is still there kickin' a stain on the groond. 'Right, mate. Where's the guys?'

'They're doon at the grit pitch.' We walk towards it. Me an ma pals got a fight planned. They Calder cunts are after The Woods, the wee bit of trees tween us an them. Us is Westburn. Calder is full a fannies, like. No danger they're gettin The Woods fae us. That's where we smoke an bag off wi birds. They tryan take it fae us every coupla weeks like, but they've no managed tae.

See, these fights didnae actually start cos a The Woods. They started when one a they cunts threatened my mate Stevie. See, one a them came up tae Stevie when he was wi his wee sister in the swing park. Stevie didnae ken who he was so he told him tae fuck off. The Calder cunt didnae like that very much an went after Stevie's sister. An Stevie went fuckin mental. Nae fuckin wonder. I dinnae hink the Calder guy was actually gonna hurt his sister, more just tryna wind him up. But here's a fuckin tip mate, dinnae wind Stevie up. He's radge. It's no a good idea to fuck wi him, like. After that wee incident, we been fightin Calder all the fuckin time.

We're almost at the grit pitch. I see the rest of the boys. Stevie, Johnny, Alan, Teish, Greig. We're at them the noo.

'Alright, guys?' I say.

'Alright?' they answer. We wait. Stevie is hopping fae foot tae foot. I see some Westburn girls at the swing park close tae us. Stevie sees me lookin an elbows me.

'Even better. Looks like we got a audience, boys.' He smiles. 'I'm gonna bash that cunt,' he sings. I laugh. We all know who he means.

'Mates,' Teish says. We look at Teish an he's lookin behind us. We turn around an see a group comin towards us.

'Here we go,' someone says. We get in a line. The group is closer.

'Right,' Stevie steps in front a us an points. 'None a yous better run. Dinnae fuckin run. You fuckin fight, right?'

'Aye,' Teish says. He's annoyed, he doesnae like someone sayin he'll run.

'Good.' Stevie turns back roond. 'There he is, the wee dick. I'm gonna kick his fuckin heid in.' Stevie points, but we know the guy. The rest a us start pickin who we're gonna fight. They're nearly at us the noo. The girls are closer, tae.

Stevie cannae control himself anymair. 'Let's fuckin get they cunts,' he yells. He runs tae the big cunt an swings. I dinnae ken what happens cos I'm runnin tae. I find some cunt I fought before.

'Alright, mate?' I say before I swing. I miss an he hits me. I see stars an I go mental. I dinnae ken exactly what happens, but I'm on top a him an he tells me tae stop. I get off him an kick his heid. He stays doon. I look roond at everyone else. Stevie'll no need ma help, he's smashin that cunt. I see Alan fightin some radge an another one walkin tae him. No fuckin danger. I run tae the second cunt. He doesnae see me till I'm already there. I swing at his stomach. He goes doon. We keep fighting till one of the Calder boys yells an the whole lot runs away. The rest a us get up an get together again. Some a us are beat to fuck, some of us arenae.

'Deek ma knuckles, mate.' Stevie shows me his hands swellin up with some blood on em.

'That's mingin, mate.' I take out my fags an light up. Alan an Johnny do the same.

'Gies one,' Stevie says. I gie him one an Johnny an Alan gie everyone else one. We walk towards The Woods.

'Did you see the big massive cunt wi the brun hair? I kicked his cunt in,' Teish says.

'Aye, right,' Billy yells. 'He was fuckin killin ya, mate, till I got there.'

Greig says, 'Did you see the fat ginger dick? I smashed him, by the way.'

We're at The Woods now smokin oor fags. The girls are walkin tae us. I recognise all a them. There's Tracy, Karen, Leslie, Lee, Alison an Jen. I'm no so good at talkin to birds. Karen is tidy like but I dinnae ken what tae say tae her. So I smoke another fag.

Stevie doesnae have a problem wi talkin to the birds an he's right in aboot it. He starts actin oot the fight, makin all these mental sounds an that. Teish takes another fag aff me an we watch Stevie an smoke. We're all mates, but me, Teish, an Stevie are oor own wee group.

Teish watches Stevie an laughs. 'He's mental like. But he's a sound cunt.' He keeps watchin, but I think he's lookin at Lee now instead. Teish fancies the pants aff a Lee. He's no as shy as me, but he's no like Stevie either. Stevie turns around an sees us lookin at them. He turns back tae the birds.

'Lee!' he shouts.

'Jesus, Stevie, I'm no deaf. You dinnae have tae shout. What are you on aboot?' Lee asks.

'Will you bag off wi my mate? Teish fancies you.' He speaks normal now.

'That cunt,' Teish whispers to me, but he's excited. He stands up mair an touches his hair. Lee looks past Stevie at Teish. She looks him up an down then looks at Stevie again.

'Aye, Teish is tidy. What, the noo?'

'Aye. Hey Teish,' Stevie shouts at Teish but Teish is already walkin tae him. Teish an Lee talk for a minute, then walk tae The Woods. Lucky cunt. Some a the other birds bag off with some of the mates. Now there's only me, Stevie, Fraser, Alan an two a the girls, Karen an Leslie. We all smoke some mair fags before it gets dark.

'I gotta go hame, mates, my Dad'll go radge if I'm no there.' I put oot my fag an put my jumper on that I took aff after the fight.

'See ya, Rab.'

'Later, mate.'

I walk hame slow. I like this time a day. It's no cold but it's no warm either. I wonder if ma big sister Susan is hame yet. She's usually oot with her pals till tea time as well.

I'm hame in ten minutes. I open the door an hear Ma an Dad in the kitchen. They're shoutin at each other real loud. I dinnae stop tae listen, I just go upstairs an maybe Dad won't ken I wasnae hame yet. Susan is already in our room, puttin nail varnish on.

'That's mingin, can you no open a windee?' I kick aff my shoes an jump on ma bed. Ma will call us doon for tea in a minute.

'Och, shut up, Rab. It's no that bad. But if you dinnae like it, you can fuck off.'

'Aye right. You cannae hear them goin at it? I'm no goin doon there.' I jump higher until my head is almost touchin the ceiling.

'Ah ken. They've been at it for ten minutes. I dinnae ken what aboot. Rab, go an do me a favour an paint my left hand fer me.' Susan shakes the pink nail varnish at me. I jump aff the bed an paint her left hand fer her. I done it loads a times so it's fuckin perfect, like. As soon as I finish, Ma shouts up the stair.

'Susan, Robert. Your tea's ready!'

Susan pushes me onto the flair an runs down.

'CHEEKY BITCH,' I shout an chase her. We race to the living room an sit in our usual spots. We come in too fast an Ma shouts at as.

'Dinnae run in here, for fucks sake! You want me tae spill your tea everywhere? You can eat it aff the flair.'

'Sorry Ma,' we say together. But we're still laughin. We stop when Dad comes in. He's ragin. We ken better than to wind him up. We eat our tea, mince an tatties, an watch EastEnders. Ma an Dad arenae speakin tae each other. Everythin is fine till Susan chucks a bit a tattie at me. Ma an Dad dinnae see, so I chuck a bit back. She kicks me an we're both tryin no tae laugh. She keeps windin me up till Dad finally sees.

'Youse better knock that shit aff,' he says. I can tell he's no bein funny so I try no tae get into it wi Susan. We finish our tea an watch telly. EastEnders stops playin an Susan kicks me again. I try tae kick her back but she moves an Dad sees us again. He stands up an now he's in front a us.

'WHAT DID I TELL YOUSE?' he yells.

'Och, Dad, we were-' I try tae say. But I cannae finish cos he hits me across the heid.

'DAD,' Susan yells. He'll no hit her, so she can yell at him. Just cos he wouldnae doesnae mean Ma wouldnae.

'SUSAN. Watch yer mooth or you're gettin one an all,' Ma said.

Dad is still standin in front a me. 'Robert, go up tae yer room, I cannae be arsed with you the noo.'

I dinnae say anyhin, I just go up tae my room. I'm no daft, no like Susan. I dinnae wantae fight. Every cunt is always fightin. Me an my mates are fightin they Calder cunts all the time, Ma an Dad are always fightin, everyone on the telly is fightin all over the fuckin world. Why does everyone need tae fight all the time? I lie on ma bed an wait for Susan tae come up. There's suddenly lots a shoutin. I cannae hear what they're sayin, but I think it's everyone shoutin. After five minutes, Susan comes up tae the room. Her eyes are red, she was greetin. I wait till she wants tae talk. I dinnae wanna upset her mair. She doesnae say anyhin for a while. We muck aboot until it's time tae sleep. Ma came up later an told us tae go tae bed. She turned the lights oot an left. There's a light fae outside that's comin in through the windee.

'Rab, you up?'

'Aye,' I say.

'Do you ever hink aboot other people like?' She sounds half asleep.

'What do ya mean?'

'I mean, do you hink other people fight like this? Hittin each other an that. Shoutin all the time.'

I think for a second. I know Teish gets it at hame sometimes. Alan an Johnny tae. 'I hink so. Maybe no all a them, but I hink it's pretty normal like.'

'I dinnae ken. I hink other people in the world arenae like this. I hink we should go somewhere like that, where they dinnae hit each other an shout at each other.'

'Aye, maybe,' I say, but I dinnae mean it. I hink everywhere is the same. I dinnae ken what she's on aboot, goin somewhere else. Like where? We'll no leave, this is our hame. Aye, it's shite but the world is shite anyway. I hink aboot all ma mates an the birds an my Ma an Dad when they're happy. Nah, I dinnae wanna leave. I'm hame.

The Sloan Prize is awarded annually for a prose or verse composition in Lowland Scots vernacular to a matriculated student or to a graduate of the University of Edinburgh of less than three years' standing.

profiles

Alice Gray is currently in her final year at Edinburgh College of Art where she has been studying for her BA in Painting, Her work is heavily driven by drawing and the act of mark-making is fundamental in my work. I work primarily with graphite and liquin. She can be reached at grayalice93@hotmail.com.

Alyson Kissner graduated from the University of Nottingham with a First Class in English and Creative Writing where she also worked with Jon McGregor on his literary journal The Letters Page. A Canadian abroad, she's on a postgraduate scholarship for poetry at the University of Edinburgh. Alyson can be reached at her twitter handle (@alykissner) or by email: alyson.kissner@gmail.com.

Amani Al-Remal completed her undergraduate degree in English Literature at the University of Edinburgh, and is now studying Creative Writing at the same university. She is currently working on a collection of short stories and hopes to write full time. Amani can be reached at: amanialremal@gmail.com.

Angela L. Hicks: Originally from Warwickshire, Angela studied Scandinavian History in London and Sweden before deciding to pursue a career in writing in Edinburgh. She primarily writes children's and young adult fiction, often drawing on the mythological and legendary influences of tales she studied in her undergraduate degree

Ashley Rauls is an MSc student at the University of Edinburgh, where she focuses on fiction writing. She holds a B.A. in English literature from Furman University. After spending a semester in London, she was inspired to write her first novel, which is currently in progress. Ashley can be reached by email: ashleyrauls@gmail.com.

Azra Tabassum is a student at the University of Edinburgh. She is currently pursuing an MSc in Creative Writing in poetry.

Cecília Giannetti is a Brazilian lawyer and writer of short stories. She is currently an MSc student at the University of Edinburgh and is working on her first humorous novel in English. Cecília can be reached by email:ceciliacatisti@gmail.com

C.M.A. Hudson is an Edinburgh MSc student and a graduate from the University of St Andrews in Fife, Scotland. Originally from Washington DC in the United States, Hudson has also studied at the University of Iowa and Kenyon College. He can be reached at CMAHudsonWriting@gmail.com.

Daniel Shand is a Creative Writing PhD at the University of Edinburgh where he also tutors Scottish Literature. His debut novel Fallow will be published in 2016. @danshand.

Dominic Hale was born in Blackpool and lives in Edinburgh. Poems recently appeared in the Edinburgh Review and the Morning Star.

Eben Diskin is a student at the University of Edinburgh. He is currently pursuing an MSc in Creative Writing in fiction. Eben can be reached at ebendiskin@gmail.com.

Florence Vincent is a Creative Writing PhD student at the University of Edinburgh. She grew up in London and has been writing professionally since the age of 20. She has previously worked as a storyliner and scriptwriter for the BBC, and two of her plays have been staged in Edinburgh and in London. She is currently writing her first novel.

Gwydion Roberts comes from Wales and is an MSc student at the University of Edinburgh. He is currently taking a break from a career working abroad with the British Council and is working on his first novel.

Heledd Owen is in her final year at the Edinburgh College of Art where she is studying for her BA in Illustration. She hopes to continue illustrating alongside a career in care work. Her artwork can be found at heleddowen.com.

Ignacio B. Peña is an MSc student at the University of Edinburgh and is a native of Los Angeles, California. His stories have been published in Headland and in The Harpoon Review. He is a first year contributor for The MFA Years, and is currently working on his first novel.

Jacqueline Thompson is reading for a PhD in Creative Writing at The University of Edinburgh, having gained her English MA (Hons) and Creative Writing MLitt from The University of Dundee. Her publications include The Scotsman, New Writing Scotland, Gutter, New Writing Dundee, For A' That (Dundee University Press) and Double Bill (Red Squirrel Press). She was shortlisted for the Grierson Verse Prize in 2013.

Jt Fels, once a Missouri-based editor, is now pursuing a Masters in Creative Writing at the University of Edinburgh. With experience in directing and screenwriting, his focus lies in the strengths of visual storytelling. Jt is currently writing the script to his first serial television drama as well as a new comic book series inspired by the pulps of the 1950s. Contact Jt via twitter @JtFels.

Kelly Pierce is a current MSc student at the University of Edinburgh after receiving her Bachelor's degree at Fairfield University in Connecticut. Her first published short story was featured in the University of Findlay's journal Slippery Elm in 2014. She enjoys writing coming of age stories and is currently working on her first novel.

Krystal Foster graduated cum laude from The University of Tennessee with a focus in Anthropology. She has since been spotted earning a Masters in Poetry at the University of Edinburgh. Although her academic focus has changed, her topic of study has not. She is curious and enthusiastic about most things on the exception of bad writing, bad people, or centipedes.

Lauren Pope is a Creative Writing PhD student at the University of Edinburgh. Her writing has appeared in numerous journals and online publications. She is the recipient of a Greenberg Poetry Fellowship, an Orkney Writers' Bursary, and the Grierson Verse Prize.

Lori Sheirich received her B.A. in English Literature from the University of California, Berkeley. She worked as an editor in educational assessment for fifteen years before deciding to return to school. She is currently an MSc student in the Creative Writing program at the University of Edinburgh.

Madelyn Harris, hailing from the sunny shores of California, graduated summa cum laude from Azusa Pacific University with a Bachelors Degree in English. Now, she has traveled across the pond to pursue a Masters of Creative Writing degree at the University of Edinburgh. She has presented her work nationally at the Sigma Tau Delta English Convention and her stories have been published in The West Wind. She is currently writing her first novel.

Marianne MacRae is a Creative Writing PhD candidate funded by the SGSAH, researching the use of talking animals in poetry. She has been shortlisted for the Bridport Prize five times and most recently her work has appeared in Edinburgh Review and Popshot Magazine.

Mark Wightman is an Edinburgh native. After what seemed like a lifetime working in media technology he is now pursuing an MSc in Creative Writing at the University of Edinburgh. He can be found on Twitter @mark_wightman.

Pauline Jérémie holds a degree in English Language, History, and Literature that she completed with distinction at the Université Paris Diderot. Originally from France, she moved to Scotland to attend the MSc in Creative Writing at the University of Edinburgh where she works on writing that often explores gender, sexuality, and feminism. She can be reached by email at pauline.jeremie@gmail.com.

Peter Mayne is a native of Buenos Aires, Argentina, and is working on his first novel. He studied English at the University of Miami and is now currently pursuing his Masters in Creative Writing at the University of Edinburgh.

Quentin Scobie is a young "multi-media" person who has yet to do many of the things that he feels might come to define him. He would like you to send him an email on quentinscobie@gmail.com if you like the thing he did and would like to receive more things he has done or will do.

Temi Oh received a BSc at King's College, but was no closer to unlocking the secret of consciousness or to synthesizing love in a test-tube. So after graduating she packed up and pursued other dreams. She married her high-school boyfriend, moved out of a city that she loved but didn't love her back, and enrolled in the Creative Writing MSc at Edinburgh.

Teresa Lee is a native Londoner currently completing her MSc Creative Writing on scholarship. She loves to write contemporary fiction and has blogged about her adventures in Switzerland, China and now Scotland. Teresa has also written a radio drama, Modern Gods. She can be found on Twitter @teresalee18 or http://teresaclee.wordpress.com.

Zoë Ramsey graduated from the Virginia Military Institute in 2012 and spent the following years travelling the world and teaching English. She's lived in over six countries and speaks a few languages. She currently lives in Edinburgh with her boyfriend and two pet rats where she tries to incorporate her travels and her rats into her writing.

THE UNIVERSITY
of EDINBURGH